UNQUENCHABLE THIRST

UNQUENCHABLE THIRST

Fleur-Anne

iUniverse, Inc.

New York Bloomington Shanghai

UNQUENCHABLE THIRST

iUniverse books may be ordered through booksellers or by contacting:

iUniverse
1663 Liberty Drive
Bloomington, IN 47403
www.iuniverse.com
1-800-Authors (1-800-288-4677)

ISBN: 978-0-595-50743-6 (pbk)
ISBN: 978-0-595-61632-9 (ebk)

Printed in the United States of America

CONTENTS

Preface vii

Introduction... ix

Chapter 1:   Meeting with the Master 1

Chapter 2:   Enchantment... 5

Chapter 3:   Lisbeth's Children 8

Chapter 4:   Moonless Night... 10

Chapter 5:   The Group 16

Chapter 6:   Recruiting.. 21

Chapter 7:   The Ultimate Test 25

Chapter 8:   Warnings 29

Chapter 9:   Breaking Loose and Letting Go 31

Chapter 10: Return of the Wandering Child.............................. 33

Chapter 11: Stones on the Road... 36

Chapter 12: Integration... 40

Chapter 13: Death and Rebirth... 45

Chapter 14: Everything Comes in Threes...................................50

Chapter 15: The Inheritance 61

Chapter 16: Official Integration and Celebration 68

Chapter 17: The Noose is Tightening 72

Chapter 18: A Sudden Turnaround 81

Chapter 19: Liberation 89
Conclusion 93

Preface

This book talks about love, courage and authenticity. Love as in exaltation, love for the other, the kind of love that blinds you, brings you out of yourself, heartbreaking love when children are at stake, love for one's self, most often held back and condemned but which finally found its way of expression through Lisbeth's exceptional life energy. Because Lisbeth is a wholehearted woman, a queen of hearts, so to say. And even with her heart broken with rejection, abuse and multiple sufferings, she could regain her own light and power because she finally followed her instinct, her inner voice, addressing her from deep inside, from her very soul, and inviting her to choose Life, to choose herself.

From then on, her journey was one of a fighter, faithful to her ideals, filled with authenticity and courage. For it takes courage to recognize the facts while avoiding the many snares of victimization, doubt and self pity. It also takes determination to search and find within her the sources of the mishap which led her to being abused and submitted, to finally choose to regain her own empowerment and live her life proudly and light heartedly.

The rest is a lesson of truth, love and vision. For Lisbeth, to assume, understand and become aware of such an experience was the beginning of an authentic rebirth. When I first met her, six years ago, she was in severe anguish and deep distress, not to mention her complete physical exhaustion. Her intense emotions were overwhelming, overflowing, yet bringing her to wonderful breakthroughs of awareness and understanding. In the process, she was attentive to her body language, she welcomed her emotions and most of all, she followed the way—and the voice—of her heart through her soul. Her determination, her persistence, her faith and her thirst for life guided her steps on the road to this wonderful healing.

What a pleasure it was for me to sustain her in this return at the source, **her - own** source. While recuperating control over her life, Lisbeth offered me the best reward ever: she allowed me to be the privileged witness and accompanying guide of the emergence and full expression of the unique human being she really is.

February 2008
Manon Verrette, Intervener and Coach, Energy harmonization/Memory integration

Introduction

Beloeil, South Shore of Montreal, 1982. Having survived heartbreaking experiences and a few years of spiritual emptiness, Lisbeth, a thirty-seven year old woman, now feels the need to find a way back to her inner self and to God. Hoping to get the help she needs, she knocks at the door of her parish rectory. The priest listens to her somewhat distantly as she tells him how she sought a career as a singer. His words are harsh and makes her feel wretched, cheap and guilty. He considers that, as a mother, she shouldn't have gone that way. Even though she tells him how she craves spiritual peace and harmony, he dismisses her quite coldly and she goes away, her spirits low, her thirst unquenched.

After this disappointing encounter, Lisbeth still returns to church a few times, hoping to find some of the solace she used to feel there. But now, the ritual ceremonies seem cold and aloof reminding her of her own inner feelings of emptiness and she remains unsatisfied.

Determined to find some kind of relief, she searches further. She always loved to sing and since this hobby had often helped her through rough times, she decides to join the local choir. After a few rehearsals, she finds it doesn't fulfill her expectations: she wants to feel encouraged to develop her talents and to share it with the community; she wants music to communicate to her soul. But the gossip is making her gringe, and she feels nothing in common with the others; for them, being in a choir is something to pass the time away, a hobby, a show. That's not what she was looking for. She feels deceived and she keeps wandering and pondering, wondering when and where she would meet someone who would lead her to the Source where she can finally quench her spiritual thirst. So help her God!

Lisbeth separated from her husband six years ago and since then, she has been the sole supporter of their three children. Four years ago, she met Steve, a brilliant pianist, and they fell deeply in love. Believe it or not, at the slightest touch of his hand, she melts in his arms. He is THE MAN of her life, regardless of the distance, regardless of their difference, in spite of everything. He also swears she is the woman of his life and she believes him. From the first encounter, they've shared breathtaking moments. Beside having a common passion for the beauty of life, for art and culture, they also have the same thirst for happiness, both earthly and spiritually. It is heaven on earth when they are together.

Unexpectedly, after five months of passionate dating, fervent correspondance and ardent phone calls, he breaks off their relationship in a letter. When she reads his words, Lisbeth is totally shocked. It seems impossible to her that such a strong love should end and the reason he gives to break off simply makes no sense to her! She believes that they are still deeply in love with each other. Lisbeth feels completely destroyed, hurting deep in her soul, in her whole being. The pain is so untolerable that she loses control over herself. In a matter of seconds, she snaps out of reality in a dark bottomless precipice. When she wakes up again, she feels as if she just bounced back up and is now holding on to the side of the abyss, unable to get on the firm grounds, and afraid of falling again. Fortunately, she finds the strength to call her psychotherapist who comes to her rescue and helps her back on her feet.

But the letter is still there and it still hurts. Steve's words are like a sword in her heart. She cannot believe it! He cannot be homosexual! Their physical encounters were so sublime, so grand, so … sacred! How can this be possible? But looking back, she starts to realize that there were some hints about it. She just didn't want to see them. Even now that he openly reveals the other side of him, she still has a hard time to figure it out. And she cannot let him go. She calls him back and he accepts to remain friends with her. They keep in touch regularly and get together sporadically, always with the same overwhelming intensity.

It is through Steve that Lisbeth met Louisa, a thirty year-old teacher, friend of Steve's mother and sister. In no time, Louisa and Lisbeth discovered they had a lot in common and they started to correspond regularly. Louisa lives in Noranda but often comes to Montreal. During one of her trip, she calls Lisbeth and they talk for long hours. Louisa tells her new friend that she is meeting with a spiritual guide and that she has found what she had longed for all her life: a comforting friendship and a spiritual support with complete acceptance of who she is. Louisa is so enthusiastic about it that her overflowing energy reaches Lisbeth deep in her heart. It's now beginning of June and when school year is over, Louisa is coming to stay in Montreal for the Summer. She has a job with her new friends and she will call Lisbeth as soon as she settles down in the city. She promises to ask her spiritual guide to meet Lisbeth.

Until then, Lisbeth does not want to build up her expectations. Her life must go on. She has a job as a translator/revisor for an editing house and she is expecting a legal settlement to get her share of the estate she owned with Ralph, her ex-husband. She has been called to appear in court on July 27th. Since the lawyer, the husband and the assets are all in Ontario, she'll have to travel there and, for the first time since she moved to Beloeil with her children, she'll have to face Ralph, their father, the man she married and shared her life with from 1964 to 1976.

Just the thought of that brings her back to Hearst, where she lived for 22 years. In this small town, she was well-known and appreciated, both as a person and as a singer. She even gave five excellent concerts as a soloist and the response was overwhelmingly enthusiastic. Many people told her she was losing money and time not using her talent to make a living. She had always wanted to use this God-granted gift to serve Him only but this comment worked its way through her mind and she decided to move to the Montreal region to start a career as a singer. Being unaware of the immense competition she would find in the metropolitain jungle, she soon found out that she had but flimsy chances of becoming a star. It was difficult to even get a platform where to sing and the bars became her concert halls. Reality rapidly caught up on her: at that moment, she was thirty-five, mother of three, working with an unexperienced young organist and, above all, she refused to comply to certain stereotyped demands like sleeping with the manager. Her physical appearance did not fit the standards of starhood? Maybe! But she was not going to become anorexic in order to have some illusory success! After four months of struggle at a very low salary, she decided to quit, leaving Mark, the young musician, struggling with his career with a new experienced singer. This was yet another heartbreaking disillusionment for Lisbeth and she cried out in poetry, writing verses to express her deception. She had a beautiful dream, vibrant as a concerto, luminescent like the sun, as colorful as a rainbow and filled with love like an endless romance … but the dream soon vanished and her bright sky turned to grey, bringing her abruptly back to reality.

All she had were the wonderful memories of her short singing career, the two summer months the duet spent entertaining the clients of the Mon-Chez-Nous Hotel near St-Jovite, in the Laurentians. Despite Mark's irritable and irritating temper, these days were sublimely ecstatic and remain her best souvenir of her piano bars' life. The duet benefited from the excellent fine cuisine, and had a spacious summer cottage on the lakeshore of the beautiful Lac des Plages all to themselves where they could relax. And the clientele was fantastic, appreciative and sophisticated, mostly composed of rich cottage owners from Montreal. The musical duet were requested to come back the following summer but since they were not working together anymore, this was another impossible dream!

Lisbeth is now working full time, revising and correcting interesting books in a quiet room, on the second floor of the Editing House. She tried to accept her situation, recuperate from her heartaches and go back to her 'normal' life of a single-parent. A big hole in her bank account is all that'sleft from her too-short artistic career. How could she fill that hole? Her wages are barely enough to survive with her three children and, with the father paying no alimony whatsoever, she seriously was thinking of going bankrupt. That would really be the easy way out and would bring her relief from her financial burden. But that would also include losing her dignity and leaving her brother with part of her debts, since he co-signed her loan at the bank. No, really, she can't do that; she has to find another way out … and she's counting on the settlement of the court for her share of the marital estate. Let's hope it comes soon.

Beginning of July, Louisa is back in Montreal and she calls Lisbeth. Again, Louisa's overwhelming enthusiasm stirs up Lisbeth's desire for spiritual accomplishment. Louisa reports that she meets regularly with Martin. This man is just back from India where he studied and meditated under the wise supervision and guidance of a master; he wants to share his oriental philosophy with those willing to lift up their soul through purification to face the final Return. As Louisa puts it, Martin's rules are quite strick and rigid: no drugs, no alcohol, no meat, no sex. But Lisbeth considers it as a normal condition to initiate oneself and be part of the chosen people of God. She has no problem with the absence of drugs or alcohol as she never took any. And who needs meat since it can be replaced by some other kind of proteins. It's just a discipline to acquire, a peak to climb, an ideal to attain.

As for the 'no sex' part, Lisbeth considers that to be her real challenge but yet her sex life with Steve is ambiguous. He is the one and only who brought her to the highest peaks of ecstasy; he is the one and only who touched her deep inside her heart, spirit, body and soul; the one and only who met the feminine and extrasensitive being sleeping inside her. We could say he is the Prince charming who woke up the Sleeping Beauty. He is the only one who had the privilege of Lisbeth's complete surrender. He is attentive, loving, delicate, charming, gentle, vivacious and affectionate, oh so tenderly affectionate, the kind of qualities Lisbeth always looked for in a man. It's seventh heaven with him, it's cloud nine in his arms and Lisbeth can never forget that. It is stronger than all the deceptions, heartaches, sufferings, long periods of silence, abrupt departures and uncertain returns. Would she be able to resist him if she joins the group of spiritual travelers under Martin's guidance? Would she be able to stop singing those inspired songs she wrote and for which he composed the music? That is the big question. Because she felt happy with him, she felt in complete communion with him physically, emotionally, musically, spiritually. She is certain they are twin souls.

CHAPTER 1

▼

MEETING WITH THE
MASTER

Finally, Louisa has arranged a meeting between Lisbeth and Martin. Lisbeth has butterflies in her stomach, hope in her heart, but at the same time, she wants to consider this rationally. First, Martin tries to explain that the discipline he requests from his followers comes from India but Lisbeth's main concern is: "Who is Martin's Master? Who does he follow?" Looking far beyond the room, Martin remains silent for a moment and then says: "My Master is Christ!" Did he read Lisbeth's mind? Those are exactly the words she wanted to hear! Her breath is taken away, she feels she has found what she has longed for, she is so relieved! She readily opens up on the subject of sexual continence; without hesitation, he assures her of his help to go through the hardship of withdrawal. Lisbeth is then ready to follow the leader. But Martin holds her back saying she should take a few days or a few weeks to think it over, stressing the fact that it is a serious commitment.

A bit surprised by this forced delay, Lisbeth has a hard time finding some sleep. She admires Martin for having the wisdom to give her time, time to commit. But she is now unconditionally fascinated by this sublimation adventure. Deeply impressed by the words: *Christ is my Master*, and feeling a persisting call from her soul to reach something higher, something she names **the Absolute**, Lisbeth calls Martin and they make an appointment for Sunday, July 25.

With some apprehension and strong palpitations in her chest, Lisbeth rings the doorbell. A man with a gray beard, his head completely bald, a severe look in his eyes, invites her in. She enters a bare living room; the incense scent, the flickering of candles appeal to her. There are no chairs, no couch, just some low tables with statues, and a stereo player. The Master is sitting on a cushion, his back to the wall and she sits in front of him.

He asks: "Where do you come from and what are you looking for?", Lisbeth spontaneously discloses herself and tells him about her marriage with Ralph, about how she discovered soon after his dependency to alcohol, the three children they had together and finally their separation, and the Church's nullification of their marriage. She then tells the story of her meeting with Steve, the love of her life, and the shock and bewilderment she felt when he broke off their relationship, telling her he was gay. How baffling and impossible it was for her to believe this since he was the best lover she ever had. Though they still keep in touch with each other, Steve is now in a serious relationship with a man and Lisbeth is totally free and willing to live this ascetic discipline Martin is asking..

All through this Martin listens attentively, interpreting and analyzing all she says about her past life and her actual quest. He also works with numerology; she knows nothing about this 'science' but she is captivated by the results. Martin tells her about her mission on earth: according to what he sees, she is the only person who can save Ralph's soul and Steve's soul who both are on a destructive, non-evolutive slant. This touches her heart and soul so deeply that she starts to cry: she has finally found her true objective in life, she accepts the responsibility and is instantly determined to accomplish this God-given mission. All her doubts evaporate. She is one with the Master.

She would do anything to save Steve, her one and only love. It might not be easy but he's worth every effort. Steve is a privileged human being, with tremendous talents and potential, and overflows with energy and joy. And now, he is facing an ultimate choice: to join the homosexual world or to embrace the heterosexual identity. Lisbeth is ready to give up a large part of herself in order to recuperate Steve to God.

Concerning Ralph, the mission is not so clear. Martin told her that, considering the situation she was in, as a mother, she had no other choice but to run away to save her children. That, she understands very well. But how can she save him from himself? Through Martin's comments, she understands that she also has a dependancy toward food since she is overweight. She thus comes to the conclusion that if she controls her 'hunger', she will somehow be able to save Ralph from his 'thirst'.

Martin also explains to Lisbeth that, in this life, we have to atone for our misdeeds. In other words, we have to amend by paying our 'karmas' in order to purify ourselves and be clean and ready for the next incarnation. Lisbeth feels a karma mostly towards Mark, this young musician who filled the emptiness left by Steve's first departure from her life. The relationship between Mark and her never was harmonious and remained almost secret because of their age difference: he was 18, she was 34. Of course, Lisbeth suffered playing the cruel game of indifference not to reveal their love in front of people. But, recalling some part of her psychotherapy, she realized that she had simply made a transfer of her love from Steve to Mark. Being older than him, she felt responsible; consequently, she ended their love relationship and let him go. Still, his well-being was important to her; they now meet occasionally as friends only. And especially now that she is serious about the whole process of purification and spiritual growth, she is even more motivated to be honest with Martin.

After this first conversation, Martin leads Lisbeth into another room across the hall 'to meet the group', he says; and he leaves her there. She expected three or four people, as she had deduced from Louisa's talks. Surprise! She finds herself in the middle of the room with about twenty young men and women, all sitting in a circle on cushions or directly on the floor. She is astonished, impressed and ill-at-ease. She instantly wants to leave but she is awe-stricken and immobilized … Her stress alleviates a bit when she can spot her friend Louisa among the 'crowd'. She is requested to introduce herself to the group and as she does it, still standing up, she feels very self-conscious, knowing they can feel her discomfort. Then, someone invites her to sit down among them. They take turn introducing themselves and they start questioning her in the same way Martin did when he first met with her: "Where do you come from?"–"What are you doing in life?"—"What are you looking for, here?" She answers briefly, going easy on the details; after all, it's just an introduction.

Towards the end of the meeting, she is invited to share her impressions about this group she abruptly joined without notification. She feels distraught, a bit perturbed–how can she can predict what will come out of this in the following months! Is it on purpose that Louisa had mentioned just two other persons as being Martin's followers? Or is it just because they are her favorite friends among the group? Lisbeth decides to stop analyzing and pondering. She firmly decides to follow this road of purification, whatever the cost, even if she has to live the process through the group, she shall do it. This is her salvation, this is her mission.

Chapter 2

▼

Enchantment

Being part of a group is a big huddle for Lisbeth but apparently, she has successfully overcome this first obstacle and she tries to cope with it, trying to get to know each one of the members. Unaware that so many people from so many different cultural levels were following Martin's guidance, she now sees it as a sign that his teachings are good and worthwhile. He discovered his philosophy in India where he spent eighteen months fasting, meditating and studying with great masters of Hinduism and Buddhism, mainly through the teachings of Sri Aurobindo and The Mother. It is then and there, so says he, that he discovered his mission: to share these lessons of wisdom. To Lisbeth, this seems such a noble mission and she recognizes his competency to spread the oriental philosophy in the Occident.

Completely under the spell of this first encounter, Lisbeth still must attend to her financial affairs; she leaves Beloeil to appear in court in Northern Ontario. By mere chance, Mark travels with her to visit his parents. They travel by bus leaving early in the morning. All along this eighteen hours ride, Lisbeth shares her enthusiasm about her new spiritual process and her young friend grasps her every word as a Word of God. She indeed feels inspired and believes the Holy Spirit is acting through her; she is even astonished to hear herself express things she had never even thought of before and which appears to be a revelation to her and to Mark.

At times, she strongly feels Martin's presence, as if he was travelling with them in spirit. She is amazed!

In this magical state of wonder, she feels herself merging with Mother Nature and realizes that the sun flooded her with its light, warmth and energy all through the day. As dusk sheds its veil, the stars multiply in the sky and the golden moon-beams fill her with vibrant feelings. She is overwhelmed as she tells Mark: "This day has been so full of gifts that only one thing could add to it: some spectacular northern lights." Well, believe it or not, no sooner has she finished her sentence that Mark, looking out the window, gets up and exclaims: "Look! There it is!" Getting up too, Lisbeth indeed saw the beauty! The dark sky was clear with the most beautiful dancing aurora borealis! Lisbeth's eyes fill with tears of wonder as she admires the celestial splendor of the phenomenon: she compares it to a bride's long veil floating in the wind, glazing and sparkling with diamonds (the stars). Her heart sings a prayer of thanksgiving for such great marvels in life and in her life.

At the end of his trip now, Mark addresses Lisbeth: "I have this bizarre feeling that I'm making a 'return' trip!" Lisbeth understands exactly what he means: she also has the impression of bringing back home, as a grown-up, the child she 'kid-napped' three years ago. Of course, she did not kidnap him but he was so young and so naïve about the future! And he thought his life in Montreal was going to be a happy merry-go-round. He is now twenty-one and the next time he leaves his family, Lisbeth hopes he will do it on his own, and be totally conscious of his choice. As far as she is concerned, she completely released him and she is not going to interfere in his life.

He disembarks in Timmins and Lisbeth goes on alone, lost in her thoughts. She feels so unburdened now and she thanks God for this. She had enough rough times in her life already, so many responsabilities to shoulder all alone and she appreciates this lightness, a short break before meeting Ralph tomorrow in court. How she wishes he won't show up! Nevertheless, she feels strong enough to see him and to treat him with respect as long as he keeps a certain physical distance between them. She knows what to expect—he'll grab her, hold her tight and then, he'll either want to kiss her or hit her. She clearly prefers that he stays away from her.

As she's pacing the floor in the Law courts' hallway, she's trembling in apprehension, feeling repulsed. She is aware that Ralph is very sick: he has been hospitalized a few times for a severe cirrhosis of the liver and, even though the doctors tell him he should stop drinking, there is no way he can. He is past the point of no return and he often loses track of his own life. Lisbeth knows that this legal settlement takes place against his will as did the process of nullifying their religious marriage. But her request is very small compared to what she could have had of the marital estate. And that's all right with her: when she left him, she took the children with her, away from him and accepted to carry the complete responsibility of their well-being. She would never have left without them!

When she mentioned to Martin that Ralph never paid alimony for his kids, the man had this strange reply: "I understand that he doesn't want to pay ... I wouldn't either. You married him to be fertilized and have children and then, you stole them away. You used him selfishly; you took a part of him and you ran away. Now, why would he pay?" Surprised by this macho statement, she considered it quite improper and decided to disregard it. She now concentrates on the settlement of her case once and for all.

Suddenly, she hears a loud familiar voice echoing in the staircase of the huge stone building: Ralph has arrived. Her heart beats so fast but as she sees his silhouette disappear at the end of the hallway, she can now breathe. A few minutes later, her lawyer tells her that Ralph won't appear in court because he walked right in during another case, interrupting the Judge who made him sign the papers and advised him to go back home. Sad situation but she's so glad she won't have to see him! All is well that ends well.

This settlement is quite meager, just a few thousand dollars, but enough to finish paying Lisbeth's car and a small bank loan, a great help in easing her financial burdens. As she travels alone back to Montreal, she now feels she can close that chapter of her life, and go lightheartedly towards her new-found mission, and her new life with the Master.

CHAPTER 3

▼

LISBETH'S CHILDREN

Lisbeth has three children: Vicky is 17, Sarah is 15 and Yann is 12. Vicky, a vibrant, easy-going red-head, has just graduated from Beloeil Secondary School and is preparing to attend a Montreal college to study Printing and Graphic Arts. Sarah, a beautiful outgoing brunette, has quit school to work with a traveling Circus. Of course, Lisbeth was not happy about that as she would have liked to hold her fragile and vulnerable dove in her nest for much longer. But she knew that Sarah was so fed-up with school that she would have failed her grade and that she was determined to leave, with or without her mother's permission. So, Lisbeth blessed the young bird and let her try her fragile wings in the wind. Lisbeth also wanted to keep the door open for a possible return of the prodigual child in case the wind turned. Her maternal heart was hurting but she knew her child needed this freedom, or at least this illusion of freedom.

And Vicky, a determined young lady, was also preparing to leave the nest and she encouraged her mother to let both of them go. Did she really understand the difference between their destination? Being only fifteen, and very fragile healthwise, Sarah was going to work with a circus, mostly outside, rain or shine, traveling from place to place, sleeping in trucks, trailers or tents, eating hot dogs and fries, drinking soft drinks or whatever else, among strangers, to earn a few miserable pennies, not knowing where she will be the following week and what not. Isn't it enough for a mother to be worried and reluctant? It's different for Vicky who is seventeen, in good health, and who is going to share an apartment with her boy-friend and two other friends while studying and living on student grants money ... isn't that more comforting, even if it's in Montreal, the big city? I let you consider the situation and ponder. Luckily for Lisbeth, Yann, this brilliant and mature twelve year old boy, is staying home; and being very clever, he sure will comfort his mother.

In order to help Vicky, Lisbeth decides to give her the bed she's using now and to buy herself a new one. She mentions this fact to her counsellor, Martin. What an unexpected reaction he has! With an authoritative voice, he retorts agressively: "What? You want to transfer all your 'trips' to your daughter? You want her to live what you lived? What kind of vibrations is there in that mattress? No, no and no, it's senseless. You have to burn this mattress."

Astonished but wishing no harm for her children, Lisbeth accepts the severe verdict, considering it as another step toward purification. She will burn the mattress and buy a new bed for Vicky. As for herself, Martin suggest a 'tatami', a straw mat, symbol of ascetic practice and renouncement. She buys a double-sized tatami and places it on the wooden base her father had made especially for her. To make it a bit more comfortable (she's not used to sleep on a hard surface), she covers it with a couple wool blankets. And all is well. Except for the weekends when Vicky comes back home, Lisbeth now lives alone with her son, Yann, who is really mature for his age and very successful in school. Over all, Lisbeth loves her three children dearly and she is very proud of them. Though her heart aches for Sarah, Lisbeth is confident that all will be well as she follows her new direction, feeling more and more light-hearted.

CHAPTER 4

▼

MOONLESS NIGHT

Regular correspondance and occasional long distance phone conversations keep Steve and Lisbeth in close contact. Three years after their first separation, Steve came back to her and they travelled together from Montreal to Vancouver. It was a wonderful trip, as enchanting as a honeymoon. Since then, they continued their romance and, in August, Steve is coming over in Beloeil to spend a few days with Lisbeth. Being aware of Martin's presence and of his influence in her life, he considers the possibility of joining the group. Though Lisbeth is ecstatic about Steve's trip to see her, she is also quite apprehensive about spending these few days in such close contact with him. Considering she wants to respect her new rules of life, she perceives this as an ultimate test, a great challenge.

Her *first* initiatory trial was the group. She got used to being part of a group and now she feels comfortable with them. The *second* test was becoming a vegetarian. Except for a few cravings for meat, she keeps it up and she appreciates the weight loss it brings along. *Third* test: the pallet, the straw bed, but that wasn't difficult: she can easily endure physical pain without complaint. *Fourth* test: sexual abstinence. Of course, she is attracted to men but it's generally very easy for her not to succumb to their physical offers. With Steve, it is different: she never could resist him. Now comes the greatest test. When they finally meet, they talk about it and, to Lisbeth's great relief, Steve accepts this restraint. Thank God!

However, during the first night lying in bed beside him, Lisbeth feels so vulnerable. She calls upon the Virgin Mary to cover her with a chastety blanket because the temptation is so near and so strong! Steve approches her with such tenderness, he's so gentle, so comprehensive, so sweet! And to her great relief, he respects Lisbeth's choice even if it means continence for him too! She perceives this as a proof of his love for her.

On the second day of his visit, he drives Lisbeth to Martin's place for her weekly session. He will come back to get her in about two hours. Martin knows that Steve is visiting with his other pupil, Louisa, and he would very much like to have him among his disciples. Through his talks with Lisbeth and Louisa, Martin is aware of Steve's great potential and he considers that Steve would be a precious stone for the fortress he wants to build. But Steve is not ready to join; he might wait for the next round, he says.

During their meeting, Martin decides to change his routine: he uses music as a background to their encounter. Is he aware that Lisbeth is very sensitive to music? Does he know that Steve is a professional pianist and that, with Lisbeth, they shared hours of music and songs? Does he do it on purpose or is it just a coincidence? Nonetheless, he makes a selection of classical music and asks Lisbeth to lie down on the tatami and to relax to the sounds she hears. Martin sits on the floor at her feet and watches her reactions as she lets herself be carried away by the melody and by Martin's occasional comments.

She is not really aware of it but the music has a strange effect on her; she seems to be under some kind of spell. The part played by the piano touches her deep inside; the choir brings tears to her eyes; the strings play on her nerves and the brass instruments irritate her ear. The oriental sounds carry her away in another world. At times, she feels as if she is being lifted up while her center (plexus) is held down on the floor. She barely hears the phone ring and is a bit surprised when Martin picks it up. She feels he shouldn't answer the phone during a therapy session but she figures it must be important. And since he talks very low, she easily remains in her state of concentration and meditation. At the end of the session, when she's ready to leave, something has changed in her. She is in a strange state of well-being, somewhat zombie, floating, in a daze, as in a dream. Whatever caused this unusual condition, she wouldn't even think of asking.

In the meantime, Steve was meeting with Louisa who is very fond of him, to say the least. They share a real friendship but she is most likely in love with him. One thing is sure, she is charmed by him and by his natural magnetism. Steve being so significant in her life, he is an important subject in her conversation with Martin and today, she is bringing him a gift from the Master. Indeed, Steve receives a miniature ivory Buddha's charm, symbol of purity and rebirth, that he'll have to wear as a necklace for a whole year. This talisman is supposed to protect Steve and to save him. "When two women league together to save one man, says Martin, I just have to join in and do something!"

During the first half-hour, Steve thought Louisa was the same as she used to be, lighthearted, communicative, smiling, attentive to his words and in total admiration for him. Then, she left for a few minutes to make a phone call. When she came back, Steve noticed a huge difference. In no time at all, Louisa had become completely detached and cold. Whatever happened during those few minutes he couldn't fathom.

When Lisbeth joins them after her meeting with Martin, she feels a strange ambiance. Steve is puzzled by Louisa's attitude and expresses his relief to see Lisbeth and hopes she'll be able to put things straight again. But this moment of hope is very short-lived because he soon notices that Lisbeth is also different, as if on another planet, far away, inaccessible. He feels she's now a stranger, in her way of being and in her language. She cannot explain it but she also feels out of this world, outside of herself. She is there with the love of her life and she feels nothing. She notices the fact but she is completely unable to get out of that state of stupor. A gigantic wall has built up between her and Steve. Could it be Martin's action? Is it possible that, through the music, he subdued Lisbeth to his will power? And the phone call he answered, was it Louisa? And would he have used the same hypnotic technique to act on her too? Lisbeth tries to rewind the cassette in her mind to find some clues to this puzzle. She is now sure Louisa and Martin were talking together about Steve but she is also convinced that it is for the good of the three of them.

Steve, being very sensitive, intuitive and perceptive, sees beyond the masks. Keeping his cool, he gently tries to recuperate Lisbeth to him but she seems to be fading away. He is deeply hurt by this sudden indifference, not to say coldness. Late that evening, while having coffee in Lisbeth's dining room, he decides to play his highest card. With his most sophisticated and sincere words, with the deepest feelings of tenderness and love, he proposes to Lisbeth. It's an ultimate declaration of love. Touched deeply in her heart, overwhelmed by Steve's beseeching sincerity, she starts to cry. Her tears are coming down in a cascade with the same intensity as Steve's flood of words. He has turned on the waterworks of her soul and it's pouring down her cheeks, through her fingers, along her arm as she's holding her head, and down to the floor. Yes, a stream from her heart to the floor. With her other hand, she is holding the hand of the man who is her greatest love ever and who could be her husband now, if only ...

For so long, she had dreamed about this ultimate moment, she had waited and hoped for it to happen! Why is it that now when the time is here at last, she is so tortured by it, as if she's split in two, right down to her soul? Steve never saw her in such a state of confusion and he still doesn't understand what is going on inside her. He has no inkling of her inner battle. She is flooding with pain, with sorrow, with contradictory feelings, and the stream is so intense that it's even wetting Steve's hands and clothes, and filling the space between them. He is kneeling down in front of her, wondering what is causing this overflow. One thing he knows, it comes from deep inside her and it's been blocked for a long time: the sluice gate has just broken open.

Tears of joy, maybe, for the long expected declaration and request! Tears of regrets for having to turn down the demand! Tears of deception for the 'fiance' who thus refuses to follow her on this new purifying road! Tears of self-pity for the happiness that could have been! Ultimate tears for her own life before the severe but liberating rules of the Master definitely close in on her! At this moment, she is lost in all those assumptions and cannot figure out which is which. She's crying, and crying, and crying, and she cannot stop it; yet her heart seems cold, untouchable, unreachable, as if it was beating in another person's body. They talk, they share sentences, they try to understand each other but there seems to be no way out.

It must be four o'clock in the morning when they finally go to bed. They still reach for each other and hold tight in a warm embrace but their tenderness is now bitter sweet. No moon, no stars in the sky! A long black veil has spread over their unique and overwhelming love. It is a deep dark night!

When the new day comes, it's time for Steve to return home. As always, she lets him drive her car and, while they're heading for the train station, even if she feels as sad as can be, her eyes are completely dry now. Her body has been totally irrigated, but her soul is desperately crying, her heart is tearing to pieces and she's in real pain. The sky is gloomy and Mother Nature seems to be in the same mood as Lisbeth. Indeed, at the zenith of the day, the sky is as dark as the darkest night and a heavy rain is falling. The wind suddenly starts blowing so violently that the car swings on the pavement. Visibility is almost nil, thunderbolts rumble loud and lightnings strike hard, tearing the sky open. Lisbeth and Steve have never seen so many elements break loose at the same time. Nature is expressing loud and clear what the couple is feeling deep inside, a devastating torment.

As they arrive at the station, the rain stops as suddenly as it came. It's now time for their farewell kiss. Steve approachs Lisbeth and softly, holds her against him. These past few days have been a terrible trial for both of them and this moment is the last ordeal for Lisbeth. With whatever strength and courage she still has, she tries to stop the electric vibrations from going through her body, wanting to resist Steve's embrace. She feels this is their last kiss and she would like to imprint it forever in her heart. She would like to melt in his arms and abandon herself for a few seconds to their infinite love. Steve feels her momentary weakness and pushes her back abruptly. And with a bitter tone of voice, he tells her: "Oh no, you won't give in now that I'm leaving! Don't do that to me, I wouldn't take it. Not now!"

Lisbeth is shocked and instantly retracts within herself. She also realizes that she was not the only one fighting back her natural pulsions. His sudden rejection gesture hurts and her whole being contracts as she backs away from him. And she says to him: "No, no, it's okay, I'm okay!" He then opens the door, exits the driver's seat and grabs his suitcase in the trunk. Running in the puddles of rain to cross the street, he rapidly disappears in the building to catch the next train. Lisbeth sees him fade away as if he had turned into a phantom and she's not sure if he's heading home or somewhere else to hush up his pain.

Lisbeth now feels so empty, so terribly alone, alone with her inner storm, and tired, oh, so tired of this inhuman battle! How is Steve going to react? Is he going to try to run away from himself? And what about her? She feels lost, completely lost in her feelings right now! But being who she is, she acknowledges the choices she made and she suddenly feels proud of herself for not falling prey to the ultimate temptation. Driving back to her home, alone in her car, she decides to close this chapter of her life, leaving the past behind; but still, she looks forward to meeting Steve again as they planned. In September, they are going to get together in Rouyn-Noranda for a family reunion at his mother's home. Louisa, who is almost part of the family, is also invited and she'll be there. Meanwhile, both Louisa and Lisbeth will go on their journey under the direction and teachings of the Master, both individually and with the group.

CHAPTER 5

▼

THE GROUP

In his sessions with his disciples, Martin also works with the energy of different stones and he has already given Lisbeth a crystal pendant that she wears as a necklace. So as to alleviate their burdens and become members of the Sixth Race, the one and only that will survive the Apocalypse, the disciples are encouraged by the Master to free oneself from sentimental attachment and negative influences and vibrations. In order to follow the teachings of the leader of the Chosen Race, Lisbeth lets go of some of her jewels, starting with the ones from her years of marriage with Ralph. She had already sold her engagement ring to one of her sisters and given her wedding band to her daughter Sarah; but, according to Martin, that was a mistake and he wants her to get them back. Whatever the cost, she is determined to follow the rules and she takes them back with the promise (from Martin) to hand them back later in a different form. The disappointment of the two girls is discernible but Lisbeth is impervious to it and she gives these two pieces of white 18k gold to Martin. He will melt them to purify the metal and shape it anew before giving it back to Lisbeth "when the time comes", he says. She also gives him the lovely double row rainbow crystal necklace she wore at her wedding, a dazzling black crystal necklace and a ravishing gold chain with an encaged cultured pearl. Plus, plus … many other precious objects.

On an every day basis, Lisbeth is faithful to her meditation sessions, another prescribed rule to be part of the group. She experiences some difficulties but she works hard to overcome them and fulfill her duty. She lies down on the floor or sits up in the lotus position and slowly articulates the vowels with emphasis, sings the notes of the musical scale, trying to perceive each sound, each vibration, and projecting her voice from deeper to louder and higher. Since she loves to sing, she enjoys these exercices and they help her reach her inner self. The next step of the routine is arduous: stretched flat on her back, with her arms spread out so as to form a cross with her body, she breathes slowly and deeply for five minutes, concentrating on the light of her third eye to welcome and track all the images traveling on her mental screen. Afterwards, she faithfully writes down in her journal her personal thoughts, reflections and musings arising during those fifteen to thirty minutes.

These daily 'reports' are analyzed during her weekly meeting with Martin. He thus acts as a kind of psychotherapist and charges twenty dollars a visit from each and every one of his disciples. Through their writings, he gets to know them very well and it helps him establish the necessary rules to lead his flock toward the main objective mentioned earlier: purification and liberation of the disciples who have chosen to form the Sixth Race which shall save humanity from complete destruction.

Every Sunday, at the group meeting, each pupil shares the events of their preceding week and, through the exchange, Martin elabores on what has to be done to correct certain situations, to recruit new members, to improve the harmony among them, to prevent excess, etc. He rules with a firm hand, oversees everything and does not allow weaknesses. From 9 to 4 and sometimes 6 no one is allowed to eat but a fruit and it must not interfere with the meeting. A few weeks ago, one more restriction has been added: no more TV, radio or newspapers; all these are judged to be useless social activities, spreading adverse influence, draining their energies out, reducing them to the lowest basic level and in Martin's language, preventing their evolution.

People in the group hail from different social classes and have different civil status. One older couple, in the forties, Claude and Claudette, have a young twelve year old daughter. They both are working professionals and have been friends with Martin for many years, even before his eighteen months' trip to India. In a way, they are his assistants. Lisbeth is the next oldest one followed by Louisa. All the others are between twenty and thirty-five; they all (but for a few exceptions) seem to have a history of drugs or/and alcohol abuse and no religious background. Most of them have no links with their parents and are clinging to the group as if it was their lifebelt. Others attend one meeting, take a peek and leave, feeling unable to follow Martin's strict rules.

Gradually, Lisbeth learns more about the origin of the group. It started before Martin's departure and included but a few members. Martin expected 'his friends' to continue their activities while he was studying and purifying himself in order to lead the Sixth Race through the Apocalypse. He had planned on being in India for two years with masters like Sri Aurobindo and the Mother's disciples. But the group didn't survive without him around and in order to save what was left of it, he felt he had to come back after a year and a half, thus missing part of the teachings he should have received. Claude and Claudette, the faithful friends, helped him to reintegrate the group, inviting old members to rejoin them. Two of them came back and the new members can feel their 'seniority' during the meetings. Overall, the group is quite ill-assorted and the task is colossal to keep it harmonious.

Lisbeth gets to know Martin a little better day by day, mostly through these early supporters. They say he had been married to a beautiful woman he passionately loved. He wanted to have a child with her, but since she was frequently and openly unfaithful, he divorced her. And he carried his disappointment and sorrow as a deadweight for many years, playing music in bars, drinking and taking drugs to forget his sorrow. One day, someone maliciously told him that he was the ANTECHRIST. This sentence threw him into a deep depression and he locked himself in his home, in complete darkness, recoiling from all contact with the world and crying his soul out for two whole weeks. Then, regaining his self-control, he decided that, if that was his destiny, so be it!

Lisbeth doesn't know all the details about the Master's life but she knows he changed his ways: he stopped drinking, taking drugs, and also stopped abusing women to become an ascetic. From the 170 kilos he used to weigh, he went down to 75 kilos with the help of a vegetarian diet. Having only a grade seven education, he acquired most of his knowledge in the streets, in books, in life experiences and, just recently, in an ashram in Pondichery, India. From this country, he also brought back numerous symbolic objects, for example the crystals his disciples are wearing and the ones decorating his meditation room along with hundreds of precious stones surrounding Hindu statues dispersed all over his apartment.

In order that each member of the group harness the same energy channel, he suggests that they place pictures of Sri Aurobindo and the Mother on a wall in their homes and arrange a small altar with incense and some symbolic objects, preferably from his collection, in a special spot reserved for meditation. Lisbeth is always obedient to all these requests and every Sunday, she is there to meet the group.

Week after week, there seems to be more and more conflicts, individually or collectively, and Martin does his best to solve them. Lisbeth often finds the time tediously long and the ambiance heavy but she believes that this is THE way and that she has to go through all this to get rid of all her 'imperfections' and attain complete freedom in harmony with the universe. And since she already experienced a psychotherapy, she feels confident; she has settled a few interior conflicts and traveled part of the road, or so she thinks.

But her fellow 'soldiers' are prompt to remind her of her weaknesses and bad habits in their scorching ways. But she is willing to pay the price of humiliation in order to reach her goal, which is to feel and touch the Absolute, the constant presence of God in her life. And it seems she found the right guide to lead her on this illumination path. Indeed, Martin considers himself as a savior, a good shepherd giving his life for his flock. As he says it, his goal is to extract the 'karma' of each of his flock and to carry it somewhere to be burned later. When he finds out that Steve slept with Lisbeth on her tatami, he is furious. Even though they did not make love and that Lisbeth considers it a great victory, for the Master, it is a fault, a violation of the rule, a feigned chastety. They should have slept in different beds. Not doing so, they contaminated the straw mattress and impregnated it with sexual vibrations. Incidentally, he finds out that Lisbeth has a double-size tatami to fit on the bed's wooden base. He summons that the box be cut to make a single bed so as to make sure Lisbeth is going to sleep alone in it from now on. Claude, his handy man, is going to accomplish the woodwork without delay. Thus entering Lisbeth's intimacy, he takes the opportunity to investigate further and, at the Master's requests, he burns some incense to chase away offensive spirits and to purge unclean vibrations from her bedroom.

Lisbeth really must be ensorcelled, in another world, in another dimension to allow such invasive conduct. Her natural self would have preserved the sacredness of her personal quarters which she always considered her own temple. So let's blame her apparent indifference to the fact that she is seriously oriented toward self-purification; this helps her overcome the pain of the invasion and accept Martin's guidelines as being part of the purification process. She believes the Master is inspired by universal wisdom and that every actual act of detachment is a step forward to attain her ultimate goal.

CHAPTER 6

▼

RECRUITING

Recruiting being part of the group's duty, Lisbeth often thinks of Mark, the young musician, as a possible candidate. He now lives with Lana who also believes he's in need of a guide. In her contact with the young couple, Lisbeth often talks about her new spiritual journey. She also expresses to Martin her friends' desire to join the group; his first reaction is negative: he does not wish to include them now. When the time comes, though, he does meet Lana alone and he discovers her desires to help Mark get rid of some homosexual tendencies. The Master again is confronted with two women wanting to save one man; he thus decides to meet with Mark and he finally accepts the couple in the group, naming Louisa as their tutor and spiritual mother.

From this point on, Lisbeth is ordered to keep away from them and to abstain from interfering in Martin's work with them. One could have think this happy event would strenghten the links between them but it's not so. Quite the opposite in fact, it is a separation, a detachment, a leave-taking. Is Lisbeth sad about that? Not really: she is too focused on the well-being of everyone and this has no price. She trusts Martin and thinks Mark is in good solid hands. She is willing to back away and she considers the whole thing as a relief, a load off her shoulders. In fact, the more she journeys on this path, the more relieved and unburdened she feels.

Martin announces a special meeting for the group on Sunday, August 30th, Everyone has to attend except for the new recruits, Mark and Lana. No excuse will be accepted. It's scheduled for 9 sharp and the members will have to vote for or against Louisa's candidacy to become a permanent member of the army of purified soldiers. Each one also has to explain in writing the reasons of his vote. In the membership process, Louisa had to meet with each co-soldier individually in order to fortify her motivations and her will to definitely adhere to this group, soon to be called *Conscious Souls Army*. Sunday morning, Lisbeth gets up early and is ready to vote in favour of Louisa's definite adhesion to the group. She gets in her car and heads toward Montreal to get to the said meeting place. To her great dismay, she suddenly finds herself on the wrong road without knowing how it happened. Struggling in her mind and with her heart beating faster than the speed of her car, she somehow manages to find her way and she finally gets to Martin's house.

Ten minutes past nine!!!! Ten minutes late! Ten minutes too late!!! The door is locked, which is unusual. Her heart beats even faster and she feels terribly embarrassed. It all happened against her will. She rings the doorbell and waits. No answer. She rings again and waits. Yet no one answers the door. What's going on? Close to panic, she is really puzzled! She feels the presence of the group inside but why is it that no one will open for her? One last try and she's ready to go back home. She now knocks earnestly on the door and soon hears the safety lock turning. Jo-Ann, Martin's young protégée, is there and gives Lisbeth a cold welcome. Bearing the Master's message, she asks Lisbeth to sit in the next room and wait for someone to come and get her when Martin says so. No explanation whatsoever.

Expressing her sincere regrets for being late, Lisbeth sits right next to the door of the said room. There, all by herself, she feels dejected, humiliated, punished for something completely blameless and out of her control. She still cannot explain to herself how she got lost and she even less understand the penalty. Down-hearted and tortured between her sincere desire to be part of whatever is going on in the next room and a strong impulse to leave this place, she ponders and tries to objectively analyze the situation as well as her mixed feelings. After making the choice to stay and wait, she calms down a bit but still finds the time terribly long. On her mental screen, she suddenly has the flashback of a specific event that took place when she was a child. Let's make it short: to punish her for being too curious, her mother had locked her out of the house and refused to open even when Lisbeth was screaming in panic and desperately banging on the door. Little did the mother know that her child was caught between a closed door and a threatening huge grass snake creeping toward her. When the mother finally opened, she sure cut short of her admonishing words and remained speechless at the sight of the exceptionally big reptile. The child quickly vanished inside the house without a word but she had recurrent nightmares of serpents attacking her for many years afterwards.

That's how Lisbeth feels now sitting in this room, locked in with her feelings, like an innocent prisoner, as if the doors of paradise had closed definitely in front of her, leaving her only with a slight hope that someone will open them and let her in. So close to paradise and yet so far! But seen from the outside, what do you think? Was it the glory of paradise or was it the tortures of hell? Around noon when she's finally allowed in, she finds out that Louisa has already been officially accepted as a soldier of the Sixth Race and has had her initiation. Lisbeth feels despondent that she did not have a right to vote for or against her friend's candidacy, not even the opportunity to give her comments on this engagement. It's only later that she will be allowed to read the formal membership text of commitment. And even then, blinded by her absolute search, she won't be able to read between the lines.

Membership and commitment of the pilgrim

The ladder you are starting to climb today cuts through the crystallizing sphere with its thousands of forms. It goes through the ever moving waters of swirling tides; it crosses the most terrible hell, pushes through the thickest maya and ends in a melting lake of blazing fire to finally reach the fire people, the Ignifugents of the scarlet heat.

Where does this ladder lead you? Where does it end?

It goes through the six sections of the dazzling spheres. It reaches the powerful throne of the fifth part and goes up to an even more powerful throne.

Who sits on the throne in the fifth section?

> The One of whom we cannot pronounce the Name, except with an absolute worship, the Youth of never ending Summer, the Light of life itself, the Wonderful, the Ancient, the Lord of Love of Venus, the Great Jumara holding a flamboyant Sword, the Peace all over earth.
>
> Pilgrim _____, welcome to the ladder.
>   (Name of the pilgrim)

For the time being, she tries to catch up with the rest of the ceremony. Martin announces that Claude is ready to go up in the hierarchy and access the next degree of the ladder. Another round of ballot will take place for this promotion but, having joined the group too recently, Lisbeth cannot give her opinion; she'll just be a spectator. Once again, she feels left out and she is trying to understand how it works, how to climb up the ladder to the ultimate degree of absolute bliss, in other words how to go up the Stairway to Heaven.

Nevertheless, she is deeply touched when the Master spreads out a large wall carpet showing a shepherd in the field surrounded by his flock and offers it to Claude as a sign of his official promotion. Claude is now equal to Martin on the scale and he will have a delegated authority in the group. The chosen one is also emotionally touched and he is crying along with his wife Claudette. Lisbeth, fragilised by the earlier events, wipes the tears that are rolling down on her cheeks. She understands the symbolism of the object and it reaches a sensitive spot within her. In the picture, she sees Jesus as the Good Shepherd and she really feels like a small sheep. She would like the Good Shepherd to hold her against His heart forever.

But for the time being, she still considers herself as a lost black sheep and she is willing to pay the price for her redemption and her allegiance to the elected flock.

CHAPTER 7

▼

THE ULTIMATE TEST

Labor Day weekend is here and, in spite of the Master's disapproval, Lisbeth is going to meet Steve in Rouyn, as planned. Friday afternoon, Steve calls her at work saying he has arrived in Montreal (from Sudbury), that he is going to take the bus to Beloeil and wait for her at Eva's, Lisbeth's best friend. Though Steve knows Eva quite well, Lisbeth is a bit surprised about this detour but she accepts readily to go and pick him up there. It's in Eva's house that the 'lovers' meet again since the last incident in front of the train station, about a month ago. How will it feel to be face-to-face again? Lisbeth seems self-assured as she salutes Eva cordially and greets Steve with a friendly hug, no more. They stop at Lisbeth's place to pick up her luggage and immediately hit the road toward Rouyn-Noranda, a six hours trip.

Steve doesn't own a car but he loves to drive and he does it well. So Lisbeth never hesitates to let him be the chauffeur when they travel together; it is granted and mutually agreed upon. All along the way, Lisbeth talks constantly and enthusiastically about Martin, about what she lives through him and among the group, and about her amazing discoveries with the teachings and meetings. She is now wearing a crystal pendant inside her blouse and a black wooden crucifix on a string over her clothes, as the Master requested. She is also wearing an interlaced belt around her waist as a symbol of chastety and asceticism. For the time being, the belt is green to indicate her first steps on the road to purification. In the course of things, depending on personal evolution, she'll ascend to a different color, to black, brown, yellow, red, blue and even white. Lisbeth doesn't know yet the meaning of each color but she can see different fellow soldiers wearing different colors.

Steve listens and questions her further; he wants to know more, to delve deeper; in fact, it looks like he wants to know everything. The more interest he shows, the more details Lisbeth gives him. And her exaltation is strengthened when in turn he explains some positive side effects of the Buddha talisman he is wearing. Her deepest desire is for him to join the group and walk the road with her; it really would be the ultimate bliss for her. Her wish is so strong that she even reveals some parts of the personal conversations she had with Martin since the beginning. Among other things, Martin got the message from his cosmic guides that Steve is the only one who can save his father and the rest of his family. Being the first-born, it is his responsibility to open the way for them and they are waiting for him to accomplish his important mission. Considering the six hundreds kilometers of non-stop conversation, they most certainly are filled with spiritual energy, or so we would think.

Nevertheless, Lisbeth is quite apprehensive when she puts down her suitcase in Steve sister's home where they are going to lodge for the weekend. Steve is uncertain of the surrounding vibrational influence as there is a lot of agressivity and strong arguments in his sister's marital life. But since Lisbeth and Steve never had an argument before, she feels confident it won't be an issue. Her difficulty is not there; her apprehension relates to the bedroom. She knows that, in spite of Martin's absolute ban, she'll sleep in the same bed with Steve. To not do so would be a supreme insult and a complete lack of trust for Steve. But how will it play out? Underneath her apparent shell of detachment, she still feels quite vulnerable, being aware that Steve has all the keys to break her open and touch her sensitive fibres. He knows her well and he loves her well, oh so well!

During the first night, since it was quite late when they arrived and they both were exhausted with the long trip, nothing special happened. A hug, a good night kiss and, cuddled up one against the other, they tried to sleep. In the shades of night, Lisbeth thinks Steve is sound asleep but he just dozes off and on, praying, meditating and wondering, just as she does. In the morning, they are going to meet Steve's family. Louisa is there too. Steve's mother and sisters gaze at the sight of the two women wearing crystals and belts and they realize both women have changed quite a bit. Of course, Steve had already noticed and now, he allows himself to react to these changes. In his opinion, it's all right to lose weight (both women were overweight), but to lose one's mind is something else. To Steve's eyes, they both seem to have lost their lucidity and logical reasoning and he doesn't appreciate. Having always consider Lisbeth an intelligent woman, he is kind of puzzled with her new self.

In an attempt to circumvent this impersonal mental wall, when they are back in the bedroom that night, Steve gets more audacious, insistant and impudent in an effort to reach the authentic woman he loves. He would really like to exorcise Lisbeth's cult for Martin's teachings. He deluges her with significant convincing arguments and gives her warm embraces, entwining her in his loving arms. She turns him down softly at first but then, with all her strength, she pushes him back, also fighting against her own desires. Would she be totally honest, she would find herself on the same wavelength and share his passionate feelings. But she prays, she implores the Holy Lady to help her be faithful to her chastity vow and to give her the necessary strength not to fall into temptation. For such is the situation to her: Steve seems to be possessed by the spirit of evil which could also grab her into his claws. As much as she longs for Steve's devoted love with all its tenderness, kindness, fusional fever and complete fulfilment, she has to remain strong by fear of falling into the eternal damnation. Such is Martin's threat!

Indeed, Martin considers that if she lets herself be caught into the swirling passion of her love for Steve, she shall be condemned to spend the rest of her life in corruption, prostitution, satisfying only her most basic instincts. The torture she feels right now is nameless, indescribable; it's worst than a rape. In fact, it's the opposite of a rape! To desire someone so intensively and not being able to reach for him! To resist and refuse the greatest pleasure, the purest and deepest joy she has ever felt! And her lover's call is so passionate, so eager, so sincere, so untolerable! Untolerable and unbearable … until everything cracks down.

Steve cannot stand it anymore. He is angry and he pushes her away with the back of the hand that was holding hers. He pronounces harsh words, as sharp as a sword, and he turns his back to her in rage. She cries in silence, completely devastated, dejected, laid up for not being laid down, violated in her thirst for love and need for tenderness. Is it through her own will that this happened or is it someone else's power acting through her? She refuses this disturbing thought in the same way she denies the fact of their first real quarrel when Steve mentions it to his sister the next day. She has started on the way to ascetic renunciation to spiritually save Steve, the love of her life, and even if it means losing him forever, whatever the cost, she is determined to fulfill her mission. But she is really not aware that another spirit took possession of her power. She is completely under the spell, unconscious of Martin's domineering power.

The next day, she leaves Rouyn-Noranda with Steve but drops him off at an intersection where he is going to hitchhike to Sudbury. When she sees him through her rear-view mirror, she has the feeling of a definite farewell. Stoically brokenhearted, all by herself now, she is traveling back to Beloeil completely anguished, powerless, empty, numb. Ignoring her pain and pushing her tears down, she tries to lighten up by singing a few significant songs. A particular one comes to her mind, a beautiful song interpreted in French by Nana Mouskouri. She sang it at least a hundred times in the past and she knows it by heart: *«Quand tu chantes, je chante avec toi, liberté ... Quand tu pleures, je pleure aussi ta peine ... Quand tu trembles, je prie pour toi, liberté, et quand tu es absente, j'espère! »*[1] The melody brings tears to her eyes and her subconcious mind is talking through these words but her feelings are too mingled and twisted at the present moment for her to get this clear message from her inner self. She'll let Martin interpret it for her when she meets with him and she knows he'll see it as being an undeniable sign of liberation. Isn't it the liberation song of the slaves *"Va pensiero"* composed by Verdi in his opera *"Nabucco"*? But tonight, even if she drives near Martin's place, she won't stop. She doesn't want him to see her face now, she feels too exhausted, demolished, dismantled ... and vulnerable.

---

1. Liberal translation: "When you sing, I sing with you, liberty...When you weap, I share your sorrow...When you tremble, I pray for you, liberty; and when you are absent, I long for you!"

CHAPTER 8

▼

WARNINGS

At work, her bosses and her colleagues are beginning to worry about Lisbeth's new friends and their integrity. They are warning her against manipulation and negative influence and they find her quite naive to adhere so easily to this group and its strange philosophy. But she is a big girl, she replies, able to choose her own way of life. Besides, this group and its leader have given her no reasons to doubt of their good intentions and if she is going astray, she trusts the Lord will get her back in the right path. Is this being reckless or overbearing or just plain candid? Whatever the case, she went through so many hardships in her life and she had the proof of the authenticity of the Words of God: *"And we know that all things work together for good to them that love God"* (Romans 8, 28) and also: *"Many are the afflictions of the righteous: but the Lord delivers him out of them all"* (Psalm 34, 19). Moreover, she is totally sincere in her walk toward the Supreme Master.

Her friend Eva is also worried; she is worried about Lisbeth's mental sanity and physical health. Lisbeth stopped drinking coffee and eating meat, that's quite all right but she has also eliminated all kinds of other foods, so what about the vitamins and essentials proteins? Eva can see her friend changing and getting weaker and weaker in many ways. Trying to remain respectful of Lisbeth's freedom and of their friendship, Eva is letting Lisbeth know of her apprehension. But Lisbeth disregards the warnings and says to herself that, someday, they'll all understand

and join her in this ultimate quest. She won't wait for them, though and she goes on her way, following the teachings and rules of her new spiritual guide, Martin.

Today, her supervisor calls her in the office and mentions that lately, she has left many errors unnoticed in the books she revises and corrects. Lisbeth is not really surprised; in fact, she herself noticed that she has a hard time concentrating and sometimes is ready to fall asleep on the job. She thinks it's due to the cleaning process in her body and that in a matter of time, she'll adjust to her new diet. She accepts the comments and promises her supervisor to be more vigilant. Yet another emergency call, but she cannot identify it as such.

CHAPTER 9

▼

BREAKING LOOSE AND LETTING GO

After he arrives home in Sudbury, Steve makes a decision and he informs Lisbeth; he chooses his love relationship with Karl, his new boyfriend, and is going to live with him in Toronto in the near future, deciding to be completely faithful for once in his life. As for his spiritual growth, he'll work on it with his own guide, but not with Martin. No further explanation, no reproach, no blame, no criticism. Maybe he'll remain friends with Lisbeth but nothing more. She receives this message without turning a hair, rationalizing and ignoring her emotions. It's not the first breaking off between them, anyway. Will she admit it hurts just the same? No, because she has closed the door to her heart and turned her back to earthly love to attain some higher ideals.

When she shows Steve's letter to Martin, he rubs his hands together as a sign of victory. "It's a closed matter, he says. Steve has made his choice, eliminating himself from the chosen flock. Next! ...—Oh! But the Buddha he's supposed to wear for a year? Oh, oh!" Considering the circumstances, Martin thinks it would be an offence to Buddha's chastety to let it follow Steve in his homosexual life. He won't let this happen and he asks Lisbeth to get the pendant back. When she calls Steve on the phone to ask him to return the precious talisman, she gets a straight 'NO' as an answer: "I received this Buddha charm as a gift from Louisa and I am keeping it". As Lisbeth reports to Martin, he just replies: "Alright then! We'll see later what we can do!" And Lisbeth is freed from this unpleasant duty.

A new phase starts in the detachment process: Lisbeth is asked to let go of all sentimental links with Steve. She has to get rid of whatever comes from him, gifts, jewels, pictures, anything that could remind her of their love and of their story. More obedient and submitted than ever to the rules of purification, she gathers all the love letters, the beautiful cards, all the jewellery, pictures, trinkets his generous lover had given her and which are, according to Martin, as many symbols of attachment, enslaving and possessiveness. So much useless weight to let go of! She now feels liberated in her walk for this spiritual pilgrimage.

Among those souvenirs, a framed painting catches Martin's attention. Entitled 'A Reflection of Love', it shows a lotus flower reflecting in the water. It's really impressive and significant. And it cannot be destroyed. According to Martin, it has to be returned to its donor: Steve needs this symbol of the love he gave to Lisbeth, he needs it to learn how to really love. Lisbeth thus wraps up this valuable piece of art and sends it back to Steve with a brief and cold farewell note. Steve responds bitterly saying he expected to get back everything he had given her.

What ever happened to the rest of the treasured objects? Oh how Lisbeth would have like to read his love letters again, to imprint them in her heart before letting them go. But, along with the rest of Steve's love tokens, they will end in the purifying fire and turn into ashes. And the story she wrote of their trip to Vancouver which he read with so much interest and emotions; and the pictures they took along the way, it's so hard to let these go. And the very first gift, her zodiac sign in 10k gold he offered her along with his love on their first embrace, how heartrending to let it go! But it will melt with other metals in the jeweller's fire and become something else.

But she doesn't want to keep an account of all the things that are disappearing from her life. Let the Master grab everything, throw it in the furnace and get it over with quickly. She's had enough suffering! Let's finish the ordeal of fire once and for all! Enough torture, enough! Still, she herself is holding back, she delays the process. She consciously keeps the beautiful shawl Steve crocheted with his own hands and heart especially for her. She also omits to mention the music he wrote and/or registered for her; she considers it a sacrilege to destroy the work of an artist and she'll keep it secret ... for the time being.

CHAPTER 10

▼

RETURN OF THE
WANDERING CHILD

It's the weekend and as she regularly does, Sarah calls her mother to inform her of her whereabouts, or more specifically of the Circus's itinerary. But this time, Sarah won't follow the ground crew. She has a cold, she says, she wants to come back home and she asks her mother to pick her up in Trois-Rivières, about a hundred miles from Montreal. End of the adventure! Lisbeth is relieved that her wandering child is coming back home and she does not hesitate to go and pick her up. But she didn't expect what she finds there: Sarah looks exhausted, weak, sick and feverish and she has lost a lot of weight. But she's not alone: Rick her young and handsome new boyfriend whom she met on the ground, is with her. Lisbeth never heard of him before but, at Sarah's request, she allows him to come along with her daughter. Back home at last, the teenage daughter is so contented she is finally sleeping in her comfortable bed. For two complete days, she hardly gets up but to go to the bathroom. She does not eat, she's delirious and she easily loses her balance when trying to stand. Lisbeth is very worried and, since she works all day, she counts on Rick to take care of her fragile daughter.

On the third day, noticing that Rick is not up to the task and that Sarah is not getting better, Lisbeth decides to drag the young girl to a doctor. She wakes her daughter up, helps her to get dressed and has to support her in her unsteady walk.

At the clinic, Sarah is sleeping on her mother's shoulder like a baby and when she occasionally gets out of her feverish lethargy, she repeats: "I don't want to go to the hospital; I want to go home!" She's in a pitiful state. The doctor's diagnostic? A very bad cold and … exhaustion! He prescribes some antibiotics and advises some rest. Sarah will sleep through for two more days.

When she finally feels a little better and is able to get up by herself, she discloses one of her project to her mother. She wants to go live in Ottawa with Rick. Lisbeth is quite surprised and questions her daughter further. Rick is only nineteen and has no real parents since he has been transferred from one foster home to another all through his childhood; he even went to reform school and to prison. Moreover, he already lived with a girl for two years. Lisbeth ponders: Sarah is only fifteen and has known him for less than a month. He is handsome, yes, but has no job, no family, no apparent drive for work. In other words, at first sight, there is no way he'll be able to take care of Sarah. As Lisbeth perceives it, this is no foundation for future happiness. Yet, she verifies deeper. While Sarah is having a nap, she sits with Rick and asks him THE question: "Do you really love Sarah?" With a hesitating tone, he finally articulates the word: "Well …", while looking on the floor. Lisbeth's doubt is confirmed but she will not tell him that. She simply replies: "It's ok, you don't have to answer me now. Just think it over and we'll talk about it later." But a firm decision is made in her motherly heart. She did let her young one leave once, even if it broke her heart, but now that she picked her back up from such a lamentable state, she won't let her child leave and be torn to pieces again.

Of course, hearing her mother's decision, Sarah cries, revolts against her supposedly unloving mother, and presents strong arguments for her benefit: "Mom, you abandoned us six years ago for your singing career and we had to manage on our own. Now, you want to regain control on us? It is too late!" Now, mother and daughter are both crying. Lisbeth recognizes her faults and promises that, from now on, she'll take care of her children and try to put things back in order. "Starting now!", she says. So, she won't let her little bird leave the nest again till she is strong enough to recognize the dangers and fly on her own. Rick can stay, though; he can find a job and let their relationship grow into love and devotion. They can see each other as much as they want. But he won't bring Sarah in a delusive world and let her be disillusioned shortly after. No, Lisbeth does not want to see her child wounded again, that's for sure. Sarah might hate her mother for a while, but the decision is firm: Sarah won't leave home now. After a few days, Rick decides to leave to find a job in Ottawa. The teenagers write to each other and communicate by phone.

After a few weeks, Lisbeth buys Sarah a bus ticket to go and visit Rick in Ottawa, as per his request. Maybe the girl expected to stay there ... maybe! But, after less than a week, she comes back home, crying in her mother's arms. She found her loved one with his pregnant ex-girlfriend and totally indifferent to Sarah. Another heartbreaking situation both for the mother and for the child. And Sarah becomes conscious that her mother saved her from an even worst deception. Mother and daughter live intense moments filled with tenderness, mutual understanding and loving reconciliation.

Meanwhile, Vicky is sharing an apartment in Montreal with her friends while going to school. But she does come back home for the weekends, and Lisbeth is eager to tell her oldest daughter what she told her second one: Yes, she might have neglected them for a while but now, she is going to be a better mother. Vicky has an honest reply, filled with joy and love: "Yes, Mom, I'm glad. But don't expect us to change overnight; give us a chance too!" It sounds quite fair to Lisbeth and she then shares the same words with her son. Yann is glad to hear this good news about his mother's new awareness and commitment concerning her parental responsibilities. He is a brilliant and successful student, self-disciplined, autonomous and quite perceptive for his twelve years of age. This a momentous event in their family life.

Of course, Lisbeth is reporting everything to Martin, her Master and spiritual guide. He is delighted and comments: "Bravo! Another family reunited through the grace of God and of the Divine Mother's love!" Martin wants to meet them all: he saw Yann once and offered to give the boy some English lessons but the young boy didn't swallow the bait and he left with a book he shall never read. As for Sarah, through Lisbeth, Martin gave her an opal ring "to give her a life because she really needs it", he said. This piece of jewellery is a temporary loan; she has to be ready to return it upon request. To Vicky, he offered to change the emerald stone on her serpent ring (Vicky's chinese sign) but when he mentioned he also wanted to change the shape of the ring, she categorically refused: "No way! You won't change my ring!" Lisbeth thought that, in his own way, Martin was trying to conquer her children to his cause.

CHAPTER 11

▼

STONES ON THE ROAD

In her weekly personal meetings with Martin, Lisbeth now talks about her childhood and her relationship with her own mother. She perceives her mother, Maryan, as a religious, almost sanctimonious, stern, domineering and hypersensitive woman who suffered a lot in her own youth and is still not too comfortable with herself and with her life. And she repeated the traumatic ways of her parents and grand-parents onto the next generation.

Lisbeth still remembers her mother's inquisite attitude toward her, always searching for some faults that, being a child, she could not even imagine. And she constantly felt her mother's judgmental eyes watching her, to the point where she sincerely thought a mother and a daughter were linked from inside, in a secret place where she herself could not even see. Lisbeth felt Maryan was spying on her, harassing her and accusing her of all evils. She perceived her mother as a policeman, who never sees the good and is always looking for a shortcoming. It's no wonder that, as a teenager, Lisbeth felt rejected, was scared of her mother and always felt guilty in front of her, no matter how good she was trying to be. Life was not easy at home and it would be hard to say which of the two women cried more tears, constantly aggravating one another, one having her menopause while the other one was living her adolescence.

When she was about seventeen, Lisbeth confronted her mother with this sentence: "I have the impression that you don't love me!" The answer came straight back: "It's not my fault if you were big when you were born!" To Lisbeth's heart, it sounded like: "That's true and you caused me such sufferings right from the start!" What a way to comfort a child in need of love! Lisbeth had heard the story of her difficult birth so many times that she registered all the pain and is now able to remember all the details. The whole process is embedded inside her. She also realizes that her mother would have had enough of four children … she is the fifth one of ten, the first one who was consciously undesired. This can very well explain (but not excuse) why Maryan rejected her; and the birth weight did not help (a newborn of 11¼ lbs is a big baby).

As an adult now, Lisbeth can deal with her mother more harmoniously and she accepts the fact that Maryan did what she could with whatever means she had to bring up her children (Five more came after Lisbeth, forcing her mother to resign herself). With therapy, Lisbeth understood many patterns she copied from her mother and she corrected more than one. She also healed from quite a few severe psychological traumas and overcame some inherited flaws. When she was young, she worked hard to please her mother and be loved by her; now, she remains who she is, whether Maryan approves or not. She got to know who she really is, who she wants to be and she gained self-esteem and self-confidence, or so she believes …

Now that Lisbeth is following a spiritual leader, Maryan is very proud of her daughter and she expresses it in a letter: "You inherited this spiritual yearning from me. I am so glad that you want to serve God's plan for you and be worthy of the crucifix you are now wearing." When Martin reads this sentence in Lisbeth's journal, he changes the word "worthy" for the word "faithful" and he comments: "God is Love; if you were unworthy, you wouldn't be here!" Martin also demands that all his disciples put in quotation marks all the words relating to God in their reports, "as a sign of respect", he says. He also requires that they write in printed letters, as he himself does, to encourage uniformity and unity. It also serves the purpose of erasing old programs before learning a new and more adequate one. For the younger generation, this new requirement is very easy, but for Lisbeth, it is quite difficult because she only learned the cursive handwriting in school. But she works hard to acquire this new discipline and her reports are always presented according to the rules. Everything is noted: activities of daily living, symbols noticed, colours seen, images of the meditations, dreams, and even wandering thoughts.

These days, Lisbeth is having some very significant dreams which Martin is always pleased to interpret and analyze. For example, one night, she sees a hermit sitting on a chair with an open book. From her perspective, she can only see his arms holding the book over his knees. Martin says: "You should talk to him because the hermit is yourself … and you're holding the book of science, of knowledge." Oh, interesting! So that is why she can only see what is in front of the hermit. She wouldn't have thought of that. She is amazed!

And twice, she dreams that someone is giving her a bunch of keys. The first dream relates to Steve's family and the other one is about the Editor's House where she works. Each time, she wakes up at the exact moment when she takes the keys in her hand. Martin explains: "It's all about people entrusting you in the invisible world with some clues you don't materialize in the visible dimension. You doubt, you are scared!" Or maybe she just refuses the huge responsibility! Could it be?

In her report, when she writes 'I try to …', Martin reinforces her with 'I am' or 'I want'. She has to learn to assert herself and to state things positively. It's a matter of Yin and Yang, Martin explains, Yin being the feminine soft aspect of a person and the Yang being the masculine affirmative side. Slowly, she is learning fragments of the oriental philosophy, for example, the symbolism of colours and numbers. In order to complete Martin's teachings on this matter, she bought herself the complete Dictionary of Symbols in which she finds some very significant clarifications. Of all the books the Master suggested, it is the only one she consults. All other ones from Sri Aurobindo and the Mother are simply forgotten in one of her drawers. She read a few pages in one of them but she didn't really understand, so she set them aside. Since she reads all day long at her work, maybe her head is unable to process more datas.

Talking about her job, the supervisor again complains that Lisbeth leaves a lot of errors uncorrected in the books. This time, Lisbeth concludes that she must be saturated of this perpetual task of reading and comparing, and it must have become too passive a work for her. She asks for a change of responsibility: she would like to progress from corrector to translator. Her request will be studied by the Board of Directors. She considers her request valid since she is quite good in translation. Her supervisor takes this opportunity to inform her that the head boss does not appreciate the way she dresses with indian clothes lately, nor does he like the crucifix constantly hanging in her neck and the braided belt at her waist. Lisbeth hears the comment but she feels immune to their silly, snobbish comments: they won't make her change her mind, she shall go on wearing them as a symbol of her new identity, with her new group.

One morning, driving to work, she steers clear of another car that had failed to yield right of way and had entered her lane illegally. Her quick reaction sent her on the shoulder of the road just in time to let the other car speed by, a few inches away from her car. What a shock! Still shaking, she went back on the road with the feeling that someone or something willingly wanted to cause an accident. She was lucky or alert enough, this time, to avoid the collision. When she mentions this incident to Martin, he has his own explanation: "The forces you were serving before want you to pay a price for leaving them. They are going to harrass you because you took a different road!" Luckily, as he says it, other forces are protecting her now.

CHAPTER 12

▼

INTEGRATION

Lisbeth is candid and open in her meetings with Martin and she wants to talk to him about Myriam, a mysterious lady who called at her work one day after reading a book published by the Editor's House. Why was the call transferred to Lisbeth? Only God knows! Myriam mentioned to Lisbeth that she has an interesting story she would like to publish and that she is looking for someone to write her biography. After a long conversation, Lisbeth agreed to meet with the mysterious lady in order to get mutually acquainted and to see if they can work together. Lisbeth went to Myriam's place a few times already, taking notes and recording Myriam's story for the purpose of writing the book when the information is complete.

To make a long story short, Myriam is a young woman who discovered God and Virgin Mary through hardships and sickness. At thirty-eight, she is medically condemned by a lung cancer and according to pronostics, she should have been dead a long while ago. As she tells Lisbeth, she experimented a few extrasensory spiritual visions after she stopped drinking, and now, since her conversion, she spends most of her time in prayer and uses her clear-sightedness to guide her clients in their faith to God. When Lisbeth asks for a card-reading, Myriam replies instantly: "You don't need that; your faith is already so deep, you need no one to read your cards!" Lisbeth is rather surprised with this reply but she concludes that Myriam really has the gift of clairvoyance and read through her directly. Lisbeth now notices on the wall the images of both Sacred Hearts: Jesus and Mary, thus confirming Myriam's devotion. The lady also assures Lisbeth that she is praying for Ralph who is afflicted with alcoholism; she knows the torture he is going through.

But one day, Myriam presented Lisbeth with a strange request that required time to ponder. Myriam wants Lisbeth to use the profits of the book to build a small chapel in honor of the Virgin Mary's Sacred Heart. Lisbeth does not feel up to the task and refrains from going to see Myriam for a while until she decides whether or not she'll accept the challenge.

Now Lisbeth wants to have Martin's opinion about the whole matter. His answer is: "Go and pray to a chapel dedicated to Virgin Mary and ask for a sign!" Obediently, Lisbeth goes to a chosen chapel and picks up a few leaflets all in different colours on a table at the entrance. She then walks to the front, closer to the altar and closer to the Virgin Mary's statue. She first kneels down in a silent prayer deep from her heart asking for a clear message to help her make a wise decision. Then, sitting on the pew, she starts to look at the papers she picked up earlier. She soon finds out that three of those leaflets are completely blank and all three are blue. The message is clear and astonishing! In the roman catholic tradition, the blue represents the Virgin Mary and since the sheets are blank, it gives space for Lisbeth to write Myriam's story. Totally overwhelmed, Lisbeth relates these facts to Martin who has nothing more to add. And she calls Myriam to take an appointment for the following week.

Lisbeth finds Myriam in great shape, enthusiastic, beautiful, and radiant. She even took off her wig since her hair has grown back in splendid brown curls. The conversation is warm and friendly. Myriam rejoices about Lisbeth's new spiritual orientation and also about the fulfillment of her utmost desire: Lisbeth will write Myriam's biography and she will use the gains as per Myriam's desire. This fills Myriam with joy. Moreover, she now is certain that the Lord has healed her in order to allow her to take care of her ten year old son until he gets to be sixteen. Yet, she is ready to accept God's will for her and if He decides to come and get her now, she is totally and joyously resigned. The more they talk, the more Lisbeth notices that there is a light emanating from Myriam, making her almost transparent.

Their encounter is so fulfilling, refreshing and touching that Lisbeth can't wait to share it with the group. She heartily tells everyone that Myriam is healed, completely transformed, dazzling like the sun, almost etherial. The group's reaction is cold and indifferent and Lisbeth doesn't understand. What's the matter with them? Lisbeth is totally puzzled: they usually are not too receptive but today, it's worst, they are scornful, sarcastic, despiseful, and seem to have closed minds and hearts. Could they be envious or what?

Since her first meeting with the group, Lisbeth has searched for a happy face among them, but never saw one with a spontaneous and true smile of serenity. Since they have to report all their feelings, she did write these personal considerations and reported them to Martin who encouraged her to share her thoughts with the group. Today, plucking up her courage, she plunges straight into it: "You all seem to be crawling under a heavy weight. What is it that you are carrying? What is it that is weighing you down so strongly? You all seem to be holding something heavy inside; why don't you let it go? Do not let yourself crushed by the group; this tremendous energy you are holding in could find a better use for the progress of each and everyone in the group. Just let it out, for heaven's sake. And then smile."

Lisbeth's words fell on them like a bomb. And each member exploded in his own way, emptying their bag of agressiveness on Lisbeth who dared speak her mind, thus disturbing their tranquillity. Shell splinters came from all directions and crossed the room toward Lisbeth:

- And what about you? Who are you? You often talk about other people in your life but very seldom do you talk about yourself! This conceited look of yours, is it there to cloak yourself or do you really consider yourself better than 'us'?

Lisbeth is confused: her timidity, her reserved attitude is misinterpreted and considered as arrogance and snobbery:

- Why do you always address Martin as 'vous' and excuse yourself when you pass in front of him? What are you looking for? Do you think he'll give you a special treatment for this?

Yes, Chantal is right. Lisbeth addresses Martin as 'vous' because he is the authority and it's a sign of respect; that's the way she was brought up and that's the way she feels. Besides, she always excuses herself when passing in front of someone, whoever it is; it's a matter of good manners. After all, she is not so familiar with everyone yet. She would like to express these thoughts to the group but Frank takes over immediately:

- The 'vous' expresses mistrust. Did you ever accept someone totally once in your life? I doubt it! You always keep a part of yourself on a safe ground, a little space for your suspicions.

And Martin pushes further:

- You are a specialist at sugaring the pill for yourself, even when you appear to look straight at something.

All these remarks, Lisbeth considers are an erroneous interpretation of her idealism, her cheerfulness, her optimism, her good humour and her openess to others. And the negative harassment keeps piling on and this time it's falling on her like the deluge. She doesn't know how to take it; she's not the aggressive type and has a late-reacting temper. Besides, she doesn't quite understand: she's been pushed to express herself, to surpass her timidity and her fears, and when she does, she's repressed and scoffed off. Unable to reply to these judgmental words, she thinks that accepting all this is part of the process of purification and spiritual initiation. She thus remains mute.

Exceptionally, one member of the group seems to be compassionate to her today; it is Claude. Up to now, he is the only one who has entered Lisbeth's home and now, he is telling everyone in what state of poverty Lisbeth spends her daily living. He mentions that the woman is in urgent needs for many things but too timid to ask. The time has come to find her a new apartment, in Montreal if possible, and to help her be more comfortable. A sudden wind of sympathy blows through the group and everyone is willing to give a helping hand, especially the men. Lisbeth is somewhat embarrassed but deeply touched and sincerely thankful. She expresses her joy and acceptance to come and live closer to them who she now considers her new family.

She suddenly feels it's now the time to renew her request to become an official member of the group. And since meeting each and everyone individually is a prerequisite for her adhesion, the process will allow her to open up and let them know who she really is. And it works both way: she'll also have the opportunity to know each one better and enter their mysterious world. These one-on-one encounters suit her just fine.

Through this process, Martin might come closer to one of his objectives: to gather his disciples under the same roof, one day, as a small community. Since Lisbeth is going to move to Montreal, since she is the oldest (or almost) woman of the group and since Martin is looking for a Mother for his younger ones, it would be a good combination. Considering all this, Martin sees it as a necessity for Lisbeth to get to know the members of her future family.

Indeed, following Sri Aurobindo's steps, Martin is looking for a Mother to help him in his task. And according to him, every woman is a manifestation of the Mother. He sees Lisbeth as Durga, who represents the intensity of the vital forces, regenerative and destructive. In time, Martin would like to give this identity to Lisbeth. Or it could be Jenny for Shiva, the conscious manifestation of the self; or Kâli, Mâyâ, Aisha or any other feminine deity.

But for the moment, Lisbeth is the one candidate he is concentrating on. It is thus suggested that they find a very large apartment for her so that a few other members of the group could move in with her. The message has been heard and the search is on.

CHAPTER 13

▼

DEATH AND REBIRTH

Beginning of October. A stormy cloud has formed over the group and Lisbeth feels it is just about to burst. Since she has never been part of the clans, she is surprised to find the meeting room filled with long faces all wearing a gloomy expression. And Martin is absent. This sunny Sunday morning seems to be a critical moment. Johann speaks up first. She is currently sharing Martin's apartment and he gave her the task of reading his 'last will' of thirteen (**13**) pages he wrote the preceding night. Each one of them knows the symbolism of the number **13**: death, resumption, rebirth. The message can be summarized in these few words:

I am dying ...

... from lack of love. You came to me and took all energy from me without giving in return, thus creating a hollow space ...
Due to lack of feeding and protection, I am exhausted ...
I thus have to go back to the dark side to search forgiveness and 'light' for all of you ...
*There is not much time left to accomplish what has to be accomplished: the delay is of **22** weeks.*

And they all know that __22__ is the number representing completion, conclusion. Of course, in the original text, many details are given concerning the faults of one, the selfishness of others, the good deeds of some, the indifference and the lack of willpower of all of them when it comes to accomplish what is asked from them. Martin explains that he is willing to die so that the truth becomes reality, that the Sixth Race can really live, not only in words, and that light can be manifested through the crystal world everyone is wearing. And if he comes back to life, his task will be even greater and more demanding. As a conclusion to his message, he choses an excerpt from Victor Hugo's literary work:

Extrait de (Extract from) Châtiments IX, Paris
31 décembre 1848, Minuit, Victor Hugo

Ceux qui vivent, ce sont ceux qui luttent;
Ce sont ceux dont un dessein ferme emplit l'âme et le front.
Ceux qui d'un haut destin gravissent l'âpre cime.
Ceux qui marchent pensifs, épris d'un but sublime, ayant devant
les yeux sans cesse, nuit et jour, ou quelque saint labeur, ou
quelque grand amour.
C'est le prophète saint prosterné devant l'arche,
C'est le travailleur, pâtre, ouvrier, patriarche,
Ceux dont le cœur est bon, ceux dont les jours sont pleins.

…

Ceux-là vivent, Seigneur! Les autres, je les plains.

Those who live *(Liberal translation from the original French text)*
Those who live are those who fight.
Their soul is filled with a clear mission shining on their forehead.
They struggle bitterly to the supreme height of their destiny.
They walk thoughtfully, night and day, their eyes shining with some sacred task or some great love ...
... They can be labourers, shepherds or artists.
Those who live have a kind heart and their days are fulfilled.
As for the others, I pity them.

Listening to this ultimate message from Martin, all his disciples are crying. They understand in what a dramatic state Martin is and the followers of the first hour know he is facing a symbolic death. Each one somehow feels guilty and is asking himself or herself what he or she has done wrong to contribute to this agony. Lisbeth is confused but nevertheless deeply touched by Martin's apparent devotedness to his flock. They all are emotional about the situation and firmly determined to be docile in the future, if there happens to be one.

The 'future' is there before the end of the meeting: Chantal symbolically gave a life to Martin and he arose again, coming in the meeting room with a new program. From now on, each one will have to pay 30$ a week (rather than 20$) for a private consultation. And each Saturday, for the next 22 weeks, the group will have to find a different catholic church to meet for a Way of the Cross. Each in turn shall take the lead of this exercice and faithfully report to Martin. The whole group is agreeable to the idea and it shall be done as requested. Yvon is in charge of finding the churches and of calling the parish priest to make suitable arrangements concerning the availabilities..

Lisbeth feels completely at ease with this special 'obligation'. In fact, it is a well-known context for her; she sang in Church for so long that she feels completely relaxed there as she lets the inspiration carry her away and sing some religious hymns. The rest of the group is enchanted to discover this side of Lisbeth and they appreciate her voice which helps them go deeper in prayer. Of course, this episode is reported to Martin who instantly turns blue with anger and does not allow Lisbeth to sing again, pretexting that her voice awakens bad vibrations inside the others and she thus is manipulating them … (How is that different from his own manipulation? How does it interfere with his work??!!).

Once more, Lisbeth is astonished: not one second would she have thought she could hurt someone with her God-granted gift of singing! Her voice is soft and soothing, and that's exactly the way the group perceived it. Why would Martin think differently, especially as he did not even hear her. Well, Lisbeth thinks, the way to purification is not evident and clear: some detours are unknown, some sacrifices are necessary, and she'll persevere till the end to attain her ideal.

Is it plain coincidence that, during one of her meditation sessions, she clearly sees this astounding image? An asexual character dressed in a long brown tunic is standing, arms outstretched, on top of a big rock. Simultaneously, the same character is down on the ground in exactly the same position and he seems to be talking to an invisible crowd. Lisbeth can only see the back of the personage. Once more, Martin declares that this 'preaching monk' is Lisbeth herself but advises her as follows: "Before delivering a message to others, you have to acquire stability and unity within yourself". According to him, the double image corresponds to duality and lack of unity and thus, Lisbeth is not ready to materialize her vision.

Lisbeth is more and more convinced that she has a special mission in this life and she wants to prepare herself adequately in order to be the instrument of 'God', through written words, just as Martin specified in his 'last will'. He also wrote that the first letters of her name 'Li' signifies internal fire; and she still has to materialize it, to make it visible to warm others up and shed a light in front of them. To help her in this process, he will get the hidden part of her out in the open by calling her with her second name, Pauline. This name carries the inside fire and it is well contained between two other syllables. It is not easy to change your name after 37 years but, according to the Master, this new name is more consistent with her real personality. Lisbeth is the name behind which she hides: Lisbeth is the charming one, the dazzling, cunning and silent serpent. Pauline is more serious, straight forward and honest. At least, such is Martin's interpretation.

It is immediately evident that, even after his symbolic death and rebirth which apparently weakened him, Martin still has a strong energy and he keeps controlling and directing everything masterfully. He sees everything, overlooks everything, inspired by his 'invisible guides', interpreting their messages in his own personal way. Bearing that in mind, Lisbeth (Oops!), Pauline is a bit surprised when he reads one of her notes and lets it go unnoticed. Yet, this statement made a lot of sense to her: "Psychological slavery is a kind of enslavement through which a great number of people give up their soul to a third party." *(Liberal translation from French)*. Pauline herself even forgot why she picked up that sentence. Was it her instinct? Was it through intuition? She doesn't know. But one thing is sure: she is surprised that Martin does not pick it up and arrange it to suit his purpose.

CHAPTER 14

▼

EVERYTHING COMES IN THREES

Today is Friday, October 22nd, and Lisbeth (Pauline) is called in the office of the Human Resources Director of the Editors' House where she works. Lisbeth expects to hear about her recent request for a promotion to a translator position and she is quite confident she'll get a positive answer. But the expression on the director's face indicates the opposite. Trying to be as gentle as possible, the director goes straight to the point: "We are letting you go for all the reasons you already know!" Indeed, Lisbeth knows them well, even more than the lady can imagine. Her financial situation never allowed her to dress up to the image of her millionnaire bosses. Moreover, the fact that she is a single parent (separated from her husband) adds to their dissatisfaction. The few recent events just offered them the right excuse to fire her.

Lisbeth is close to tears and feels like leaving the place and slamming the door. But she resists the temptation and she goes on listening to the director who further explains: "Of course, you are entitled to get two weeks notification and you will be paid for them, whether you work or not. The choice is yours but we suggest that you use this time to look for another job." So that is it! Lisbeth picks up her things and leaves immediately. She'll come back later to pick up her last paycheck.

But what will she do now? The following day, Lisbeth thinks of Myriam and decides to call her and ask to meet with her again. At the other end of the line, an unknown voice answers her and says that Myriam is absent. Lisbeth inquires further: they don't know when Myriam will be back because she's in the hospital. Lisbeth wants to know if she can go and visit her friend at the hospital but she feels that the unknown person is quite uncomfortable and doesn't know what to answer. Since Lisbeth is most probably a complete stranger to the voice, she explains who she is to Myriam. Then, another person comes to the phone and announces that Myriam passed away during the night but they don't know yet where and when the funeral service will take place; Lisbeth will have to call back Sunday or Monday to know more.

So, here she is, surprised, staggered, puzzled! Yesterday, she lost her job; today, she lost a friend; both events were unexpected and unpredictable to her. And she thinks: "If the saying: *'Everything comes in threes'* is right, what is the next thing that will happen around me?"

In the afternoon, she's scheduled to meet with the group for the usual Way of the Cross. On the way to the church, Lisbeth shares these two facts of her life. The reaction is spontaneous: nothing to worry about. She losts her job? Fine! They are all searching for an apartment for her so they'll just kill two birds with one stone and look for a job at the same time. It's all for the best and it will keep the group closer together. And since she lost her job on the 22nd of the month, 22 being the symbol of a terminal, of the end of something, it cannot be contested. No possible return!

As for Myriam, considering the light shining through her when Lisbeth last visited with her, she surely died in peace and serenity. And she passed away on the 22nd, thus releasing Lisbeth from the responsibility of writing her biography. Besides, there was no firm agreement between them and Lisbeth doesn't have enough material to do a good job of it. Lisbeth (Pauline) is sad, very sad but she remains alone with her feelings. The rest of the group seems to rejoice for so many releases while being somewhat jealous of their companion for the wide open road in front of her; no more obstacles to overcome. They consider that Pauline had it too easy, with no hard work, no special effort. Let's see what comes next.

Alone with her afflictions, she goes back home in the evening to find an important telephone message. She is requested to call back at Notre-Dame Hospital in Hearst, Ontario. She has a hunch but it is now too late at night to return the call … she'll do it first thing Sunday morning. And here she is, over 800 miles away from Ralph, her husband, father of her children, who is agonizing with very little time left to live. If they want to see him alive, it's now. Or never. Lisbeth already knows she will go with her children for a last farewell to their father.

It is Sunday and she is faithful to the weekly meeting with Martin and the group. She has yet another news to share with them. Though she is not really superstitious, she has to see the evidence: this time, the saying is confirmed: three important events occurred in her life within 24 hours. Concerning the latest one, Martin considers that, not only does she have the obligation to go and visit Ralph but, she also has to assist him and accompany him to his last breath. Even if he should survive for another six or twelve months, she should remain at his side to take care of him, thus redeeming her wrongdoings toward him and completely releasing the karma between them. Such is Martin's recommandation and the whole group agrees with him. Lisbeth trusts that this is the expression of the Will of God who already cleared the road in front of her: she has no job and Myriam died. Lisbeth now thinks that Myriam died first to prepare a place for Ralph and be there to welcome him in the other dimension.

Pure coincidence, Lisbeth's father is in the Montreal region on a business trip and he's returning home to Hearst the next day. Since he travelled all by himself this time, it will be a pleasure for him to bring his daughter and her kids to see Ralph in Hearst. Lisbeth is requested to leave her car to one of the group members and she accepts to do so. A few phone calls to advise the teachers that her children will be away for a few days, a call to her former employer to get her last paycheck and they are already to leave on Monday afternoon.

This is certainly not a leisure trip and on the way, Lisbeth prepares herself and helps her children; they have to be able to face the man who caused them so much pain. They have to forgive him deep inside themselves and be able to tell him they sincerely love him, no matter what. It is quite a heavy task for young ones but Lisbeth is sure they can do it. She lovingly reminds them that he is their one and only father who, with their mother, conceived them at a time when some kind of love was present between them. Whatever the quality of this love, it was there, it was theirs.

At the hospital, they are facing a new and shocking reality: the man lying on the bed is completely broken. Slowing coming out of his lethargy, he recognizes them and greets them individually. He seems to be happy to see them all. Lisbeth is the first one to come close to him to say hello. He then sees Vicky and greets her. Next, he calls Sarah by her name and greets her also. And last but not least, he identifies Yann and remarks how much he grew up since the last time he saw him. All three of the children remain still, at the foot of his bed, aghash to see him in such a pitiful state; this man they always knew as being strong, sturdy, almost unvulnerable, is lying there weak, fragile, confused and old before his time. They are flabbergasted and have a hard time breathing, completely over-whelmed by the damages of their father's life-long abuse of alcohol. They are well aware that alcoholism is the main cause of this early deterioration. After saying a good word to each of them, Ralph then turns onto himself and complains of all the aches and pains he is experiencing. Just before falling back into delirium, he concludes: "If you all came to see me, it must be that I am going to die!"

He pronounces this with a sudden awareness that the end is near for him. And his words fall as a sentence at the end of a long trial, heavy to carry, but irreversible. Everyone keeps silent after this, unable to articulate a word of comfort and unable to contradict such an evident statement. After some ten or fifteen min-utes, the three children are unable to bear it any longer; they feel sick and ask to leave the room. Lisbeth approves and asks them to wait for her in the hallway. She says a few words to Ralph, assuring him that they'll be back to see him tomorrow.

For the next few days, they pay short visits, the children not being able to bear the sight of such misery. But Lisbeth is convinced that, deep in their heart, through invisible vibrations, they are able to tell their father they love him, and to thank him for giving them life. At the end of the week, Lisbeth tells Ralph that they have to return to Beloeil: Vicky and Yann need to go back to school and Sarah wants to look for a job and a place to stay. As for herself, Lisbeth has to make suitable arrangements in order to be able to come back and accompany him for as long as he'll need her. It is a pledge she intends to honour, no matter what. And this 'what' is a complete mystery to her.

Back home, Lisbeth asks to meet with Martin to report on the situation. While in Hearst, she was unable to meditate or to accomplish the requested exercises or even to write down her daily occupations. She had only one picture in mind: the picture of a man in delirium tremens, partly unconscious, suffering atrocious pain on his deathbed. She did not even have the courage to touch him, his body being damaged to an unbearable degree, inspiring her only repulsion. Martin sees the picture and says that, under such circumstances, it is no time to meditate, it is time to fight. In spite of her powerlessness, she has to act in order to help Ralph be free from the negative forces destroying him. And she also has to be able to go beyond the physical form, and beyond her repulsion to touch the inside of the human being. Martin's words come to her as commands and she'll do her best to be up to the task.

In Beloeil, Lisbeth is looking for someone who will accept to take care of Yann while she's gone. She thought she could count on a neighbour who considered himself as Yann's big brother. He is a policeman with a family and Lisbeth trusts him but he turned her down saying he couldn't do that with such a short notice and without knowing for how long. A bit dumbfounded, Lisbeth replies that she understands and finally chooses to leave Yann with his sister, Vicky, in Montreal, where she'll have to find a school for him to continue his scholar year. As for Sarah, she has made some arrangements to stay at one of her friend's place. Dominique is almost unknown to Lisbeth but she has to trust her own daughter's good judgment; no other choice.

During these two days, following Martin's instructions and under Chantal's supervision, the group is helping Lisbeth to break her lease and free her apartment. Since no one knows how long she will be assisting Ralph, why should she pay for an empty place? In no time, her furniture is sold for ridiculous prices and even if she tries, Lisbeth is unable to catch up with them; they are too many and they are acting too fast. So she decides to handle only her personal belongings. While they're at it, the group is making some selective cleaning: some things will be thrown away, others will be burned, like clothes, glamorous dresses she used to wear for her concerts, pictures, sentimental objects, everything they suspect having a sentimental link with a person or a special event in her past life. She is quick enough to save her music but she'll have to let go of the beautiful shawl Steve crocheted for her with such great love. It is going to be destroyed by fire. Aw, how it hurts! But she prefers that someone else does this: by herself, she would not have been able to let go of the precious garment. As for the rest, whatever pieces of furniture not sold will be put in storage until she finds another apartment, God only knows when and where.

Lisbeth's father is watching the scene of destitution and is almost paralysed with horror. He feels so helpless in front of this invasive and devastative army apparently acting for his daughter's own good. He cannot say a word and he can't even try to stop the process; it seems irrevocable.

The day before Lisbeth and her father leave for Hearst, a call comes from the hospital. Ralph has been transferred to another hospital in Timmins, because of a severe uncontrolable hemorrhage. This brings another problem to Lisbeth: in Hearst, she could stay at her parents' home but in Timmins, situated two hundred miles south-east, she is a complete stranger. How will she manage to stay there and assist Ralph?

Martin soon finds the solution. Mark's parents now live there and Mark will ask them for their hospitality. They know Lisbeth, of course; but they don't really appreciate the fact that she 'kidnapped' their young son a few years back. He was more than willing to leave with her to get his freedom from his family's domination ... and he was officially an adult but ... Knowing the reason of this request and being generous by nature, they accept wholeheartedly. Lisbeth is a bit embarrassed but she has no other choice. She appreciates their magnanimity, and will be very quiet so as not to disturb them too much.

The next day, and for many days after, she gets up early and takes the local transportation to get to the hospital by bus. She finds Ralph agonizing, almost unconscious with scarce lucid moments when he recognizes her. He is plugged on so many tubes that he looks like a marionnette acting only with the movement of the strings. But he is still alive and experiences great sufferings. The nurse tells Lisbeth that he can receive no sedation whatsoever because his liver doesn't do its job of filtration and such medication would poison him and kill him instantly.

True, his liver is completely destroyed by alcohol and his whole body is leaking like a sieve. When he receives a transfusion, the blood comes straight out through the nasal tube. The doctors are astonished that he's still alive: he cannot eat though he feels hungry and he cannot drink to quench his never-ending thirst. Even when he swallows a small sip of water, it comes back out through the tubes. Never before has Lisbeth seen such a phenomenon. And it makes her realize even more the real damage caused to the body by long-term alcohol abuse; it is simply appalling.

Yet, she is now able to touch him and allow him to receive the unconditional love and compassion she deeply feels for him, her spiritual brother in a state of agony. When he has a moment of lucidity, she tries to talk to him and ask him forgiveness but he reacts impatiently as if that kind of speech just annoys him. So, she decides to communicate through non-verbal gestures and spiritual communion. She prays to the Lord that, at the end of this agony, He welcomes her once-upon-a-time life companion in His eternal Love. She also prays Mother Mary to take Ralph in her loving arms and carry him through the passage toward eternal bliss. One morning, while he is expressing strong rebellion and no one from the medical staff can calm him down, Lisbeth has the inspiration to sing. At the side of this man, tied to his bed in order to protect him against himself, she starts to sing low, very low, the melody of Schubert's Ave Maria, repeating it over and over again, louder and deeper each time. Slowly, Ralph calms down and seems to fall asleep. So, Lisbeth lowers her voice again not to disturb him and suddenly, she hears a deep low voice singing the melody: Ralph is singing with her.

A flush of heat comes out of her heart and she is overwhelmed with joy. Yes, it is real: in his semi-coma, with his eyes closed, Ralph is singing in harmony with her. What a blessed moment! His body is lying there helpless but his spirit catches the vibrations and the messages. Lisbeth is filled with gratitude for the inspiration that was given to her to sing. When the nurse comes back to the room, she is completely staggered to see her patient in such a peaceful state and her eyes are full of question marks; but she'll have to find the answers herself.

After a week of intensive care, Ralph seems to be at the limit of his endurance and he asks to be transferred back home, in Hearst. He begs, he implores with all the energy he has left. He seems to be more lucid than ever. After two days of begging, his request is accepted: he shall leave by plane in the afternoon of November 9th and Lisbeth will take the bus from Timmins to Hearst. Since his memory fails him most of the time, all the details are well explained to him and repeated many times to make sure he understands and feels secure for the trip.

All along her trip in the bus, Lisbeth tries to relax and rest. She really needs a break because she didn't have a chance to recuperate these past few weeks. Her mind travels in prayers and in reminescence. O, how she'd love to share those moments of anguish with her dear Steve! She thinks that it would be so comforting to rest her head on his shoulder near his heart where she could forget the rest of the world! But she cuts short those soft thoughts. She thinks she doesn't have the right to wish for his loving presence, not now, 'cause now is Ralph's last moments and she has to concentrate on this man who gave her three beautiful children.

Pulling herself back together, she finally arrives in Hearst. Once at her parents' home, she promptly calls the hospital; she is told that Ralph is not there yet but should arrive soon. When they inform her of his arrival, she rushes to his side accompanied by her mother, Maryan. Ralph is in a state of panic, almost in shock. As soon as he sees her, he yells: "Where were you? I was looking for you!" Lisbeth comes closer to him and reassures him the best she can. While holding her hand to make sure she stays, he calms down slowly and finally falls asleep, or so it seems. He breathes with difficulty and moans feebly. Nurses are busy around his bed, constantly checking his blood pressure, his temperature and his pulse. No more tubes, though; he is left to himself and to whatever energy he still has, which is very little. Lisbeth feels and knows that he won't last long on his own.

When visitors are requested to leave, Lisbeth greets Ralph saying: "Have a good night! I'll see you soon. If you need me, I'm at my parents' home; you can call anytime and if possible, I'll come right away. Try to rest now; I'll be back." She then leaves the room and repeats the information to the nursing staff, giving them the phone number where to reach her. In the evening, Lisbeth and her mother stay up late talking. And when the phone rings at two in the morning, Lisbeth hears it clearly. She was lying in bed, wide awake, meditating and resting. She already knows what the caller will say. She spontaneously gets dressed, even before her mother gives her the message, and she gets in her father's car in this freezing cold peaceful night. All by herself now, driving carefully with just a very small unfrozen spot in the windshield, she is grateful to the dying man with whom she shared twelve years of her life and who gave her three beautiful and cherished children. She really feels she is going to see him for the last time, and she already thinks of calling Frank, this special priest she knows, to Ralph's side for the last rites.

When she gets to the hospital, Frank is already there, praying over Ralph. Thanks, Heaven! The nurse called the right man. And Lisbeth joins the prayer already ongoing. Ralph is lucid and calm, so calm. He sees her and salutes her with a glance, just a slight movement of his eyes. He seems to be in a state of semi-conscious trance. His breathing is laborious, it's just as if he is getting each breath from miles away. It's hard work for him and the time lapse between each breath is longer and longer. His blood pressure is very low, the nurse tells me with signs. The end is near.

After praying a while, the priest goes on with the last rites and he gives communion to Ralph who eagerly accepts the bread. He, who has not taken a bit of food for weeks, swallows the sacred bread with no difficulty ... this is a miracle to Lisbeth's understanding. And she is deeply touched. The priest is also aware of the sacredness of the moment and he glances knowingly at Lisbeth. The young nurse is a friend of the family and she knows the patient very well. She even mentions that she is glad to be there for Uncle Ralph. She had left the room for a few minutes and is now back, checking the blood pressure for what will be the last time: no more pressure, no more pulse ... and comes the last breath! It is the end of this earthly life!

The soul is now free and the body is finally resting. The room is filled with peace, the silence is palpable and full of serenity! The priest goes on praying to accompany the soul through the passage and Lisbeth sings low with tears rolling down her cheeks, painless tears, peaceful tears accompanying the melody of the Schubert's Ave Maria! Words are unsufficient to express such fulfilment: a moment of grace, grandiose and unique, filled with faith, hope and love. A blessed moment, a moment of eternity! Unforgettable!

Lisbeth's heart and soul are overflowing with joy and she is sure Ralph's soul is in total bliss. After a life of turmoil and rebellion, he died in peace, surrounded with love, this same kind of love he searched for all his life but always was unable to recognize and accept it, that is unconditional love. Now the walls have fallen, the chains are broken ... he is forever free! And Lisbeth is sure that, at the end of this long night, the good Lord welcomes him in His Kingdom! This certitude is Lisbeth's greatest reward and it makes her forget and forgive everything else. Whatever sufferings and pains and hurts there was, it was worth it!

Before leaving the hospital around 4:30 in the morning, Lisbeth is asked to sign the legal papers; one of the doctors even asks if she would accept to give Ralph's brain for scientific research. She really thinks it's a good idea and she agrees. If it can help humanity, why not! And she returns to her parents' home. Her mother is praying while waiting for her daughter ... Lisbeth doesn't have to say: Maryan knows that Ralph is dead. And they stay up to see the daybreak. With the intensity of the moment, they just couldn't sleep, even if they wanted!

Around 7:00, Lisbeth calls in Montreal to talk to her oldest daughter, Vicky, who immediately figures out the reason of the early phone call: her father has passed away. Yes, she'll reach her sister Sarah and with Yann, their young brother, they will get ready to come to the funeral. She'll also call Claude, the good shepherd of the group, who offered to drive them to Rouyn-Noranda where one of Lisbeth's brother will pick them up. Mid morning, Vicky calls her mother back saying that Sarah is nowhere to be found. What can she do now since they have to leave at twelve? She left messages everywhere Sarah could pass by, asking her to take the next train heading North: she will leave the necessary money at Dominique's parents home, hoping that Sarah will show up in time.

Lisbeth is sad to hear that and most of all, she is worried about her daughter. Where is she? "O Lord, please find her and send her here with her family. Please, Lord, bring her back where she belongs. " Lisbeth cannot imagine one of her children missing for the last farewell to their father. Where is the adventurous young girl? Lisbeth is praying that Sarah didn't leave for another venture. And her main hope is that her child is safe and not caught in some dangerous situation. "But Lord, if such is your will that Sarah is not here for her father's funeral, as painful as it can be, I accept it. I offer this suffering for Ralph's salvation and for your greatest Glory, o Lord!"

While Vicky and Yann are heading north with Claude, Lisbeth receives another call: it is Sarah. Phew! What a relief! The poor girl is in panic: she doesn't understand the message that was left to her and now that her mother explains, Sarah is yet apprehensive to travel all by herself. But there is no other choice. And there will be some confusion. Ultimately, Lisbeth's father will have to drive to Timmins to pick up Sarah who managed the best way she could with the money she had to get that far. "But at least, she'll be present for the last farewell. Thank God!", thinks Lisbeth.

After such a day of strong emotions, we would believe that everything is now under control and that Lisbeth can have some rest. But no! Yet another phone call comes from the funeral home: the thanatopractor is unable to embalm Ralph's body because the skin is peeling at the touch of a finger when he tries to put the make-up on. He is asking Lisbeth's opinion as to how to handle such an unusual situation. The suggestion is to leave the casket closed. The choice is indisputable. This mishap, Lisbeth interprets as a blessing in disguise: that way, no one will be able to comment Ralph's pitiful appearance with expressions such as: "He looks so old!", or "He is hardly recognizable!" or "What a pathetic sight!". She prefers to have people remember him as they knew him when he was alive and well. And to concentrate on his spiritual salvation instead!

For the funeral, Lisbeth finds six bearers among her family and his friends. And she writes a special prayer that she will read herself as a last farewell at the end of the ceremony. On that unforgettable Saturday morning of November 12th, the close family members are present: Lisbeth, Vicky, Sarah and Yann are ready to bring Ralph to his final rest. But a heavy storm has blocked the roads during the night, preventing two of the chosen bearers to attend to their dedicated task. They will be replaced by complete strangers and the ceremony will take place in the strickest privacy. Lisbeth has advised Ralph's family in Europe and she's sure they join in prayers to the people present around the casket. Also due to the snow storm, the body will be buried later, without the family, when the temperature is suitable. Lisbeth again thinks it's all for the best.

Chapter 15

▼

The Inheritance

Back to Montreal, Lisbeth is looking forward to the next group meeting in order to share this extraordinary experience of spiritual joy and fulfillment she lived at Ralph's side, these last few weeks. But, for no apparent reason, the right time is always for another day. Finally, they will listen to her story just to get it over with and they express no compassion, no joy, no sympathy. And at that moment, Martin is absent. Claude and his wife are again the most commiserating. Claude having participated to the event by driving Lisbeth's children to it, and his wife being a nurse, they both can easily read the lines and between the lines. They say that Lisbeth is surrounded with a green aura representing telluric energy; and it's all positive since it is meant to be shared creatively. Lisbeth does not quite understand the meaning of the auras yet but she interprets this message as being compatible with her readiness and goodwill to build a better world.

On the other hand, the group has turned turtle! There was so many drastic changes in two weeks that Lisbeth has a hard time to recognize the ambiance and to readjust to the new ways. Some changed their names, others moved in a different place with a different partner; the newly wed couple has been separated by Martin who melted their wedding rings. It seems as though the master has become a tyrant; he even tries to control his disciples' intimacy such as a spontaneous wet dream or a chosen masturbation. According to him, these energy wastes are to be avoided and be transformed into something more constructive.

Some members have disappeared and Lisbeth will never know why and where. And she sees new unknown faces among which a young man just coming back from Tibet (we'll call him Bob) with a heavy load of souvenirs, of sacred objects (some of which Martin will destroy) and a philosophy that Martin will consciously alter through his interpretation.

Martin now proclaims himself a priest, yes, a priest having been ordained directly by the 'Divine' during his sojourn in India. He says that he lived in such purity, renouncement, asceticism, prayer and meditation that he has risen above all earthly attraction, above physical and mental restraints, thus allowing him to reach the supra-mental and astral zones where he received the 'divine embrace'. As he explains it, this supreme elevation is possible only with fasting, meditating, mastering of low instincts, overcoming one's desires, sentimental feelings and emotions. And that is where he wants to lead his followers. He was invested with this special mission and he will bring it to completion, not for his own prestige but through obedience to the 'One' who sent him and regardless of how costly it can be.

On this particular Saturday, Martin asks that the Way of the Cross be done backwards, that is starting from the fourteenth station to the first. The disciples don't understand the request but they will obey the orders. The next day, during the regular Sunday gathering, Martin explains what he wanted his followers to discover by themselves through the exercice. According to him, Christ's Passion is a nonsense because, after His transfiguration at the Mount of Olives where He was invested with His Father's divinity, where He has received the 'divine embrace', He could not suffer anymore; He could not feel pain nor could He die. Thus, he could not resuscitate either. Consequently, the mystery of the Cross is nothing more than a tragi-comedy invented by the Church to emotionally touch the christians and to better manipulate them. Such is Martin's interpretation of the christian faith and Lisbeth doesn't quite share his point of view. On the contrary, she rather feels that some extraordinary phenomenon took place on the Mount of Olives: to her, the transfiguration is Jesus becoming enlightened, totally conscious of who He is, i.e. human and divine. That is her own interpretation and she'll keep it to herself as a precious gift from above.

Back to every day life, Lisbeth has no more place where to live, her apartment having been closed and most of her furniture sold or given away. But that is not a problem for Martin who soon finds a solution: she is going to live with Mark and

Lana for the rest of their lease, that is till the end of June. Yann follows his mother and registers in a new school, the third one in three months. This one is just across the street from their apartment, so it's a blessing. Lisbeth is grateful that Yann easily adjusts to new situations; that is yet another blessing. And since the couple Mark/Lana are not allowed to sleep together anymore, Yann is going to share Mark's bedroom. The girls in one room, the boys in the other room, all of them sleeping on the floor. Are they going to get along in such a small space? Time will tell.

Lisbeth got her car back and she starts looking for a job. After a few unsuccessful interviews, she choses to ask the help of an Agency that will evaluate her abilities and capacities and find her a good job. Her résumé shows a lot of potential and talents and from there, she regularly gets calls for temporary assignment in different companies. Even if she is looking for a full-time permanent job, she accepts the short terms and always does the requested tasks brilliantly. She is appreciated and often, the same employer calls her back for another short term assignment. This way, she can at least handle her financial situation to some extent.

Meanwhile, in Northern Ontario, Ralph's legacy matters are not yet settled. A while back, Ralph had given a copy of his will to one of his French friends, J.A., but the lawyer being unable to find the original copy, that will is not legally valid. On the document, Ralph had designed his three children as his only heirs, completely depriving Lisbeth of any goods or money he can still have. But the law still considers her as the official inheritor (they never were divorced) and any amount left from Ralph's assets will be given to her. It is alright but she'll still respect his last will and give her children whatever is left of the estate after paying the funeral fees. She very well knows that Ralph never forgave her for leaving him and she never expected anything from him. She accepts his last decision and considers that the children deserve whatever amount they can get from their father. He never gave them much, so it's their owned rights to inherit from him. She is firmly decided that when the final settlement comes, she will divide it in three equal parts and her children will be allowed to use it as they please; she won't interfere. They all know the value of money and she trusts they'll get the most out of it.

Martin does not agree with her: the law proclaims her the only beneficiary and he wants Pauline (Lisbeth) to accept it. He says that, since her children refused to follow her in the group, they are not worthy of her nor of this inheritance. Such is the law and he considers it just and fair to make her the legal heir. For the occasion, Martin agrees with the law and through obedience to the master, Pauline will comply to the law. She now has to communicate this recent decision to her children.

Vicky and Sarah are not very happy about it: they are in serious need of money and they claim their rights. They explain their distress, they beg for compassion, they cry their misery outloud, hoping to touch their mother's heart but, under Martin's influence, she remains cold and unsensitive. The two young girls don't recognize their mother: the woman facing them now is not the sensitive, understanding and kind woman they know. She now looks indifferent and stoical to her daughters. And they are so sad now, not especially for the money they won't get but for the affectionate mother they are losing. "Of course, says Martin. You've always been too soft, too giving, too generous toward them. You taught them no discipline. It's time they learn the value of things with humility and respect." But the girls insist: they want their inheritance, considering that it was originally supposed to be theirs and that it's not their mother's real choice but rather Martin's influence on her that is depriving them from their rights. Pauline is almost ready to give in to their requests but Martin won't let her. He wants to meet in private with the two girls and their mother. For that special meeting, Martin also requests Claude's presence and they are both sitting on one side of a wide carpet, the two girls facing them on the other side of the oriental rug ... and Pauline sitting in the middle, both physically and psychologically. No chance of touching or reaching one another. Lisbeth is torn to pieces inside but this aspect of her is hidden, unreachable; Pauline has taken over and will not be disturbed by emotional black mailing.

What a cruel, distressful, painful encounter! The girls are crying out their real needs, presenting good arguments, and even swearing out their deep pain, trying to bring their mother back to her old self but nothing seems to reach her. She sits there in the middle, like a wax statue molded in Martin's fashion. Lisbeth despise such conflictual situations but Pauline will give in to the strongest power, that is to Martin and Claude, even when the master says that the girls are stubborn and greedy and that life won't be easy for them under those conditions. Being so, they are not worthy of their mother.

To these insulting words, Vicky replies: "The woman sitting here is not our mother. The mother we have known and loved is called Lisbeth, not Pauline.

Where is Lisbeth? Where is our real mother? It's to her I want to talk!" It's a heartbreaking call she lets out and she gets up to leave this stupid house. Sarah also gets up to follow her sister but Martin holds her back and asks her to give him back the opal ring he gave her one day. She gives it back with no regrets and she joins her sister in tears and sorrow.

If Pauline was not in that group, under Martin's dictatorship, if she was still Lisbeth, she would cry too because her motherly heart would be breaking to pieces. Sure, she could not stand there and remain indifferent to her daughters' distress. She would leave the place with them, take them in her arms and cuddle them affectionately, sending Martin packing. But she is now invested with Pauline's emotionless personality and she coldly accepts the separation and even the mutual repudiation. She is not their mother, they are not her daughters. "And in fact, says Martin, there is no link between you and your children since you didn't breast feed them". Nevertheless, a last sparkle of love comes out of Lisbeth and she asks Martin's permission to drive the girls to their home. He accepts, reminding Pauline not to weaken on the way.

Outside, standing on the sidewalk near the car, Vicky is crying at the top of her voice and pulling her hair in sorrow. Sarah is crying so much that she can hardly articulate; only one question comes repeatedly out of her mouth: "Mom, what are you doing? Mom, what are you doing?" And Vicky yells as loud as she can: "Do you want to drive us crazy?" Pauline is strongly grounded on her two feet and she sarcastically replies: "I cannot drive you crazy, you already are!" How cruel it sounds to Lisbeth's heart. But she is determined to attain the spiritual climax and if this is the way to get there, no sacrifice is too big, even the ultimate detachment from her own children. Finally, she has to force the girls in the car and they chose to sit on the back seat, thus making Lisbeth feel as a taxi driver, a stranger totally indifferent to their tears, or so it seems.

Up to now, Lisbeth was giving the girls a weekly allowance and paying some of their miscellaneous expenses. Considering that they are not her daughters anymore, she doesn't have to provide for their needs. The girls are now two orphans, without a father, without a mother, begging here and there for their survival. That's how they ended at Eva's place (Lisbeth's old friend), to express their dismay. They really miss their Mom who, under Martin's influence, became a complete stranger. Eva is deeply touched and, at the risk of losing her long-time friend, she calls Lisbeth to tell her about her daughters' call for help. She even adds: "Are you aware of the harm you're doing to your children? This situation cannot last. What do you intend to do to correct it?"

Lisbeth-Pauline remains cold to Eva's interference and she is polite but indifferent in her reply: "This situation will be settled with the concerned persons", meaning 'not with you'. When informed about this incident, Martin considers that the friendship has lasted long enough. Seven years represent the end of a cycle and it's time to courteously end the relationship. It will be done promptly: Pauline buys two small candle holders with the candles for her friend so that she sees the light (that's Martin's way of breaking up: a gift and a farewell). Pauline pays a short visit to Eva and she gives her the farewell gift without further explanation. She also returns the 'pierrot the clown' doll that Mona, Eva's young daughter, had given her and she asks that Mona gives her back the tiny shrumpfs that Lisbeth had given her. Pauline will replace them with something else because, always according to Martin, these small cartoon characters are symbolic objects representing one's inner-self and all his followers have to recuperate and reconquer this part of them instead of spreading it all over. Mona is one among the many children who will be touched by this demand. Lisbeth knows that the child will be hurt but she doesn't seem to care much; she just want to obey Martin's orders.

This same evening, Sarah calls Lisbeth to express her internal suffering and external rebellion concerning the last events. She also talks about her sister's resentment. Quite indifferent, Pauline listens to Sarah; but inside herself, Lisbeth is deeply touched. At first, they confront each other and accuse each other of all kinds of faults; then, the conversation calms down and leads to mutual acceptation of undergoing changes toward a better future. But Pauline remains domineering, or so she thinks.

When she tells Martin about Sarah's phone call, he considers that Pauline was too weak, that she should have refused to talk to Sarah. Allowing herself to listen was also allowing the sinuous serpent of sentimentality to act within her and it could very well work against her. In accepting the call, she obeyed to Lisbeth, the sentimental one and, for him, sentimental means the mental at work, the twisted brain which plays dirty tricks on the person.

Having had no comfort from Pauline, Sarah is lost and she wanders from place to place. She was thrown out of her friend Dominique's place because she cannot pay her rent anymore and every night, depending on the people she meets, she is looking for a place to sleep. Her few belongings are scattered here and there, wherever she was allowed to spend a night or two. She would like to come and live with her mother, Lisbeth, the real one, but she cannot find her. And the required conditions are, in all cases, impossible to reach, completely unacceptable to Sarah. Finally, the wandering girl will be accepted by her sister Vicky and her friends in their apartment. Even if they have to squeeze together, they'll do it out of compassion to get Sarah off the streets. What a pitiful situation! How can a loving mother become so unconscious of the pain she is causing her children? How did Lisbeth get to change so much?

CHAPTER 16

▼

OFFICIAL INTEGRATION
AND CELEBRATION

To follow-up with an old request from Lisbeth, Martin finally decides to organize a votation session to see if the group will accept her (or rather Pauline) as a fellow member. She has filled all the pre-requisite and individually met each one. It is now the right time for them to express openly their opinion and judgment on Pauline. She is quite confident because she felt no evident resistance during the one-on-one encounters. There was a small incident with Chantal and her son:— Pauline offered them a gift each to thank them for overnight hospitality, and they had accepted it (writing paper and crayons). But when Chantal brought the objects to Martin, he plainly destroyed them, considering they were used to buy friendship or complicity, or for whatever dishonest purpose. But it had been clarified and should be left behind.

Pauline's intuition was correct: they all vote for her to become an official member of this group of soldiers of the Sixth Race, the only one to survive the imminent Apocalypse. Pauline signed the parchment on which are written all the rules she accepts to follow and which seals her allegiance to the philosophy of the master. It is quite similar to the one Louisa signed last September (see chapter 6); a copy is given to Martin and another to Claude. Pauline received a few symbolic gifts and a welcome card signed this way: WITH—BY—THROUGH—HIM, these words at each corner of a triangle containing a circle with a dot in the middle. The circle with the dot supposedly signifies the Yin united with the Yang, representing the integrated and complete androgynous state reached by Martin.

Yet, the following weekend, Martin asks that the vote be cancelled and redone due to some obscure flaw in the procedure. The whole scenario is repeated and Lisbeth is apprehensive. What was wrong with last week's votation? What if they don't accept her, this time? But the results are positive and confirms her as a member of the group, just like last Sunday. Lisbeth, under the name of Pauline, is officially accepted as a chosen one among the Sixth Race. And the whole procedure just revealed Martin's mistrust toward his crew, at least that's the way she feels about the whole thing.

The Christmas Holidays are just around the corner but this year, Lisbeth does not feel the usual joyous ambiance. There will be no religious celebration for her, no family reunion, no pastries or sweets, no meat pies, no fruit cake. The rules are to be observed at all times. But, in spite of Martin's recommendations, Lana is going to celebrate Lisbeth's birthday, which is between Christmas and New Year's day. She prepares a special meal and invites Vicky and Sarah. Since Yann is already part of the household, the family is complete. It is a real surprise for Lisbeth and she should rejoice but she remains impassive. Her new personality under the surname of Pauline, is going through this special moment with no feelings, no emotions, no joy, no pain, no tenderness. But deep inside, Lisbeth is quite touched and would easily become emotional.

Mark is also participating; while Lana does her best to keep up the spirits, he watches over. Lisbeth knows that he is Martin's protégé; he is somewhat like a son for the master, the son he wished for so hard but never had. And for Mark, Martin is the ideal father since they are both musicians. Lisbeth feels that her young friend is Martin's secret agent with the mission of guarding the master's interests and watching over Lisbeth who is known to have a strong influence on people around her. She already was advised not to interfere or interact with Mark or Lana. She lives with them, shares their meals, pays more than her share of the expenses but she has nothing to say, no right to choose. Each word, every action will be reported more or less faithfully to Martin who is the only one able to distinguish between the good and the bad influence Lisbeth has on others.

On New Year's Eve, a few members of the group decide they are going to attend the Midnight Mass in one of the most famous church in town. Lisbeth decides to go with them but, once inside the Cathedral, she sits away from the group so she can concentrate and enjoy the ambiance along with the marvelous music of the organ. She feels that her motivation to attend this ceremony is different from her companions' who are plainly curious or nostalgic of the past. After going inside herself and reciting the act of contrition, she goes to receive communion and meditate on the Body of Christ she just received. Her prayer is profound and sincere.

After the celebration, the gang invite her to a friendly gathering at the home of one of them but she prefers to go back to her home while the public transport is still available. It's her first experience with this kind of transportation and she wouldn't want to miss the last metro train. In fact, she does get on the last train and when it reaches the end of the line, she waits in vain for the bus to pick her up. One hour she stays there waiting for a bus to come: the weather is mild and she feels good in this cool New Year's night. She is relaxed and uses this waiting time to assess her achievements of the ending year while trying to look forward to the new one. But she cuts short on the revision and vision to concentrate on the present moment. She feels quite confident in her first outing without her car in the large city of Montreal and she's proud of herself. At three o'clock in the morning, she even accepts to share a taxi ride with strangers who were also waiting for a bus that never came. A completely new experience for her and she feels good about it. Nevertheless, she's glad to get home and get some rest on her straw mattress.

Having worked at the piano-bar all night, Mark gets up in the middle of the afternoon and he wants to have his share of religious activities. So he invites Pauline to accompany him in a short pilgrimage in some local sanctuaries. At the Notre-Dame Basilic, Pauline is attracted toward the Sacred-Heart altar (It reminds her of Steve, her ex-lover, who has a strong devotion for the Sacred-Heart of Jesus). Following her intuition, she kneels down in front of the statue and starts praying for her sweet friend. All of a sudden, she receives a revelation that touches her deep in her heart and tears come down on her cheeks. She clearly hears: "You will never forget Steve ... he is forever printed in your flesh!" It is so right she even feels it in her whole being at this very moment. She doesn't know how this revelation will help her but it so precisely reflects her reality!

With her eyes still wet, she asks Mark to leave and to go visit another sanctuary. Without asking further explanation, he accepts and they head for St. Joseph's Oratory, on Mount Royal. She remembers that they were there together a few years back when Lisbeth placed a very special request for Mark. Today, she feels she's there to complete or correct the demand and to entirely leave him under the good care of St. Joseph and the Holy Family. And she totally lets go of all attachments to the young man kneeling by her side. To conclude their pilgrimage, they visit the Christ Child's cribs from all over the world. May this new year bring plenty of blessings to her and all her friends!

CHAPTER 17

▼

THE NOOSE IS
TIGHTENING

Right after their first encounter with Martin, Lana and Mark had to stop sleeping together. It's not so easy to be separated and to continue to live together. Lana has a hard time to accept the abstinence while Mark feels happy and even relieved. On New Year's Day, Lana can't stand it anymore and decides to go dancing (yet another activity forbidden by Martin) in a bar where she meets one of her ex-lovers. Feeling unable to continue with the group, she chooses to leave and go on with her former way of living.

This fact is officially announced to the group the following Sunday and Martin accepts her decision. But she'll also have to leave the apartment as soon as possible so as not to spread the 'negative' vibrations of her private life on her co-tenants. The master explains her choice in his own way: "Since she cannot save her own self, she'll have no choice but to extend herself in a child who will continue what she has not accomplish. She'll thus have to find a father and she'll give birth in pain and sorrow." With this new fact, the ambiance is very tense in the apartment. Lana is willing to respect the vegetarian diet but food is not the only aspect to consider when you share the same dwelling. And she doesn't want to leave until she can sell her furniture and get some money to cover at least her next month's rent, which is understandable. But the fact remains: it's not easy to co-exist when your ways of living are so different.

On another ground, and also due to the Christmas Holidays, the situation has deteriorated at Vicky's place. There are too many people in too small a place. A big argument took place and Sarah is thrown out by Vicky's co-tenants because of personal conflicts and lack of vital breathing space. Tolerance and goodwill have reached their limits and the teenager is again homeless. She knocks at Mark's door and again begs Pauline for shelter, saying that she is now ready to follow the rules and to be docile. Of course, Pauline will consult Martin about it and since Lana is soon to leave, he gives in, making sure that Mark will keep an eye over everyone and report any fault to the master.

For the time being, the three girls will share the same room and Mark will consciously play his role. This guy has become an expert at spying but he is not so wise at being discreet nor is he diplomatic in his approach. Lana and Sarah soon become friends, and one being the other's accomplice, they can easily outsmart the apprentice detective. Luckily, Lana leaves the apartment a few weeks later and it's a relief for everyone.

In the group, a new couple has just arrived. Rolland and Celina (Louisa's sister) already have a four-year-old daughter and Celina is two months pregnant. They sold or gave away all their belongings in Rouyn-Noranda to follow Louisa in her spiritual journey. After just a few weeks, their wedding rings readily join the common treasure (of melted gold) and they have to sleep in different rooms. Moreover, the father is rejected, the husband repudiated, being considered unworthy because he is supposedly in love with his daughter to his wife's detriment. He is also judged unable to provide for his family. Moreover, Martin thinks that the coming child is a master sent here with the specific mission of leading the Sixth Race and thus, he feels he has to take over to ensure the adequate protection for the mother and her 'chosen' child. Such a treasure cannot be left in the hands of an incompetent man who is resourceless and deprived from will power. Thus, Martin will accompany the mother and welcome the baby boy (Yep, Martin is convinced it's going to be a boy) as the guiding light in this dark world. Rolland is shipped to the James Bay, a far away land, to make sure he won't interfere with the undergoing miracle.

Let's talk about the 'common treasure' that is not so 'common' since only Martin and Paul, his accomplice jeweller, have access to it. Paul is a professional goldsmith and under Martin's command, he molds the gold and adds stones to correspond to whatever symbol the master desires, mostly for himself, sometimes for his adepts, depending on the accomplishments bringing them up the steps of the ladder, or on the need for strength to get there or remain up there. Most of the time, Martin is the only one to decide on the shape of the ring or talisman, or on the kind of stone needed for a specific purpose. But sometimes, he also receives recommendations for the East through the 'invisible world' as to how the handle a situation or a person or a piece of jewellery.

These symbolic objects are mostly used as a reward for an achievement or as a burden to carry in order to get stronger and more humble. For example, Martin gave Pauline an opal ring (from a ring Mark had given her long ago) to give her more strength. This kind of transformation of the jewel was acceptable considering that Mark was now part of the group … otherwise, the object would have been destroyed. Now, he just exchanged the birthstone for an opal. Where did the turquoise go? It remains a mystery! Louisa wears a ruby ring since the day she was officially accepted as a soldier of the Sixth Race and Chantal has a ring shaped as a cross, representing her faithfulness and self-renouncement helping Martin to carry this stubborn, rebellious group through the dense maya. One day, each and everyone will wear such a ring when they really deserve it but it's not for tomorrow.

During the Holiday Season, many members of the group forgot the rules and ate forbidden food, thus forcing Martin to tighten the noose a little more. Eggs and dairy products are now out of the diet. Lisbeth really finds it hard to accept this restraint: the cheese was a very energetic nourishment for her. But slowly, she gets used to the taste of peanut butter and she finds some interesting ways to get it down more easily. For example, she mixes it with honey or with a crushed banana; thus, it doesn't stick in her mouth and it's simply delicious. Soon, these new recipes are discovered by other members of the group and they all appreciate the mixtures. But not for long: Martin soon forbids both peanut butter and honey because it stirs up the taste buds and increases the appetite; and this is contrary to the rules of spiritual growth.

Up to now, they could eat duck weeds, kidney beans, and other kinds of starchy food. From now on, all cooking is forbidden: no frying, roasting or boiling. And no more bread, no more pasta, no more pita. All they have left to eat is raw vegetables and fresh fruits with a little olive oil and lemon juice on the salad. That's it, that's all. And it is Winter. But this recommendation came from the East and his spiritual masters are still guiding him cosmically. No arguing is allowed; it is as sacred as the Word of God. And you take it or leave.

In this cold month of January, the Sunday meetings develop into spiritism sessions. Martin talks to invisible beings who, through the mouth of some adepts, call themselves 'entities' and identify themselves as being malignant, powerful and from the dark side. The ambiance feels somewhat like in horror movies such as Exorcist or some similar dramas. Lisbeth never was a fan of such terrifying shows with stressful suspense and scary scenes. It is not the kind of strong emotions she is looking for and she despises this spooky atmosphere among the group. Her reaction is one of withdrawal: she turns inside herself and prays the Lord, using all her energy to fight against this invading invisible power using her companions to give some morbid messages. And often, the person used as a channel is considered as the entity itself and mistreated as such. It is an open combat between Martin and the entity. One of them names itself 'The Lord of the Ring' living in the most complete darkness and talking with a deep low voice. Another one calls itself 'The prince of darkness' that takes pleasure in hiding the truth behind heavy foggy clouds. Another one pretends to be 'the one' that shouts out some very acute screams generating illusions and fears.

Lisbeth refuses to participate to such a mascarade of evil spirits; she doesn't accept to be a channel for them nor does she want to be part of their violent fights. But during her individual meeting with Martin, she is more vulnerable and he, against her will, successfully brings her into a trance, asking her such questions as: "Who am I?" Beside herself, she answers: "You are Christ the Lord". He goes on: "What am I here for?"–"You came to save what was lost"–"How do you know that?"–"Through my mother."–"Who is your mother?"–"Her name is Maryan"– "Where does she come from?"–"From the darkness. She has travelled many galaxies to get here."–"Did she cause you to suffer in this life, on this earth?"–"Yes, a lot."–"What did she do to you?"

And Lisbeth goes on answering all the questions. She talks abundantly. With her eyes closed, she is totally at the mercy of the stimuli acting on her. She cannot see Martin, she just hears his voice which seems to come from another world, an underground world. She feels out of her body. Her physical envelope is lethargic, completely passive, empty of all energy, while her mind is traveling in some unknown dimension full of strange colors and images. Tears are rolling down her cheeks but they have no taste. She feels nothing: she is like a stream with no current, a vehicle without its motor, reacting only when someone pushes her. And someone is presently pushing her hard toward a predetermined destination entirely unknown to her. She is totally under the spell, submissive, obedient, absent, completely beside herself. When she snaps out of the hypnotic trance, she feels like an empty shell, a dry sponge. She remembers the scene as if it was a dream; and she wakes up as we wake up from a nightmare, just remembering the main characters as being Martin and Maryan. She was a spectator, apathetic and outside the screen. And little by little, the details come back to her memory. What an experiment! Will she allow it to happen again? Will she let Martin take control over her and usurp her power? Lets hope not.

In that same period, Martin finally decides to read the story of what she lived at Ralph's side before and when he died. She doesn't have to comment because she clearly wrote everything. Only one detail catches Martin's attention: the fact that Lisbeth still had some tender thoughts for Steve through the process. That, he cannot accept: "You say you are liberated from him and ready to go to the end of the spiritual path but ... you would still make a pause for him, wouldn't you? Don't you consider he caused you enough sufferings? Are you masochist or what? What do you hope for? Isn't it clear that he doesn't love you? And by the way, you don't love him either. Who is he to have so much power over you? He is a top manipulator and I would really like him to come and face me ... but he won't do it ... he knows I am the strongest. With just one sigh at him, I would desintegrate him instantly. Let him come! I am looking forward to that day!"

And Martin suddenly remembers the Buddha charm he gave Steve through Louisa. More than ever he wants to get it back because, he says, he feels the bad vibrations caused by Steve's adventurous life and he's experienced many sleepless nights because of that. He is fed up with this because it drains a lot of energy out of him and he is exhausted fighting against it. Yet, that is not the worst thing, he adds: what is more serious is the offence toward the purity of the Buddha. Since it is Louisa who handed the object to Steve, and since she has no sentimental link with him (oh, yeah???), she'll be the one to get the talisman back to its original owner.

So does Martin think ... but it doesn't work. In spite of all the efforts done by Louisa to satisfy Martin's will, the object will never come back. Louisa is thus accused of being timorous, fearful and lazy because she didn't confront Steve and force him to let go of the precious object. Martin considers she is protecting her friend Steve and as such, she is not the valiant soldier he thought she was. He even accuses her of complicity with Lisbeth, of some tacit agreement between them. The two women look at each other interrogatively: "What is he talking about? We don't even talk to each other since we are in this group!" Louisa is hurt by this remark but she feels so helpless. No use arguing with the master; he is always right.

Yet, in order to be worthy of this army to be, Louisa is ready to leave her job as a teacher; she is even willing to leave her family, her region and her home to come to live in Montreal among the group. Considering she is already spending a fortune just in traveling expenses, whether by car or by plane, sometimes by bus, to come to the meetings every second weekend, thus missing one meeting on two, she sure would be happier if she was close to the group, in Montreal, where she is sure she can find a good job once she is established in the area.

As it goes, we could have the impression that Martin is scared to lose some power over his disciples because he is now getting at the two professional dancers who were with him in his first attempt to create the army. Frank has a strong personality and Martin feels he wants to demolish the present chief to take his place. Apparently, the cat just came out of the bag and the scheme is out in the open. As a sentence, he will be returned to the artistic world where he'll have to become the greatest choreographer; otherwise, he'll be banish forever, Martin swears. Concerning Renald, the second dancer, Martin thinks he is Frank's accomplice but he is more languishing, affectionate, somewhat flatterer. In Martin's mind, the yound man also builds schemes against the master and he is not submissive to the rules or to the master. He thus will have to return to his parents with the mission to save them; otherwise, he shall be forever damned. So, from now on, the two artists will not be allowed any contact with the rest of the group. Only as an extraordinary privilege will they be allowed to meet individually with Martin to continue a necessary therapy.

Lisbeth is quite sad about this situation: she finds the judge quite severe and the penalties absolutely unfair ... but hush, she won't say it out loud. When the time of their official departure comes, though, she will present them with words of compassion and encouragement. The two rejected ones leave just before Louisa's turn comes to be judged for not being vigilant enough in her watch over them, as Martin had ask her to be. She was their artistic agent and since she was sharing their apartment on weekends, she should have been aware of their plot and she should have advised Martin about it. But she saw nothing irregular, she says. She is now considered and treated as trash, as a proud and stubborn being, and also as a coward for not getting the Buddha out of Steve's hands, or neck. So many unforgivable faults that she is not worthy to be a member of the group and she'll soon have to leave.

Considering all these rejections which are just beyond her comprehension, Lisbeth is questioning herself as to who is Martin's next target. During her personal meeting with the master, she questions him on his ways but his answer is: "You don't have to understand, you just have to accept and be trustful". Even if she considers that Martin is too strict, too rigid, too drastic, with no sense of forgiveness for so-called faults, she just has to shut up and close her eyes. In front of him, she feels so tiny, so helpless, and completely stunned. He pushes her against the wall and he often makes her admit faults she never committed and affirm to be what she is not. He provokes, he manipulates, he subdues. And he abundantly nourishes her feeling of guilt for the tiniest past errors which then appear as monstruous entities called to materialize. It is a terrible torture for Lisbeth who comes to think she is an abject, vulgar, sinful, unworthy creature. She feels deep repentance and cries over her sins; even the things she precedingly considered trivial now become huge and dramatic errors increasing her burden.

Martin goes far in repressing her; he even affirms that she is an incarnation of Satan himself, thus increasing her feeling of being a nuisance and crushing down her self-esteem. Lisbeth really feels the noose tightening around her and psychological walls closing tight on her brain. Exhausted, out of breath, helpless, she is subjected to Martin's thirst for power. At the end, she even accepts to be some evil character identified by Martin to fight against him. She is completely demolished and ashamed of herself; and she goes home like a robot, a sleepwalker, totally numb, less than the shadow of her old self. Only one thought holds her up, one deep feeling from her inner self, her true self. And she screams it out loud with all the energy she has left: "I am not and I don't want to be an evil impersonation! I want to be myself, only myself! O Lord, have pity on me! Forgive my sins and deliver me from evil! I am weak but not diabolic! Have mercy on me, O Lord!"

Her prayer is sincere! It is a call from her heart, from her soul, from deep inside her, right where she is extremely sensitive and fragile, from that tender spot where she suffers so intensely, the same tender spot that makes her yearn for liberty, the God-given right to freedom. She can feel that she has no more energy to fight: someone found the way to keep her down, taking all sources of energy away from her through starvation and isolation. She has no more strength; and she feels that only God Himself can save her now. Otherwise, she will be lost forever; she is going to disintegrate, crumbled by the powerful wheelwork of the machine invented and conducted by Martin.

He proclaims himself the master and he makes everyone feel that he is the strongest. She is scared of him, scared of his submitting power over her. And she is also scared to leave the group because she feels he could crush her even at a distance. He already did a good job by casting a few spells on her if she leaves. But what if she stays? The yoke is already unbearable, she is choking. Only a miracle, a powerful divine rescue action can get her out of that trap. Is it still possible? Or is she forever condemned?

While she is praying for help day after day, she receives a letter from her mother. Maryan was sick and came close to death. She was given the last rites and she even was exorcised because, through her high fever and delirium, she could see Satan materializing beside her and wanting to bring her in his dark kingdom. She went through hell while being wide awake and conscious; the incident cannot be explained medically. Maryan holds Lisbeth and Martin responsible for what she went through, and her spiritual guide, a good priest from her parish, suggested that she interrupts all communication with her daughter. She even goes further and repudiates Lisbeth as her daughter because she is part of a satanic cult. The crucifix that was given to Maryan by Martin was burnt through sacred fire to block and cancel the evil spell along with the occult manipulations.

While reading Maryan's letter, Lisbeth remains quite indifferent and she accepts the repudiation. She believes the authenticity of the phenomenom Maryan had to go through and she mentions it to Martin. With his usual arrogance, he explains that Maryan just saw her image in a mirror and that she was scared to death. He says that he has nothing to do with this event and concludes: "Well, another one who made a choice. You won't have to communicate with her anymore." Lisbeth easily accepts her mother's rejection as a normal consequence of her own denial toward her two daughters, Vicky and Sarah. She considers it fair and she deserves to be rejected according to the law of return. So let it be!

CHAPTER 18

▼

A SUDDEN TURNAROUND

Through all this hurly-burly of restrictions, ruptures, departures, bearing in mind her own survival and all the new aspects of her life, Lisbeth is looking for a steady job, more and more aware of the symbolic signs from above. Driving along the metropolitain streets, one of those signs attracts her attention: on a large notice board, in huge letters, she reads the word: PRONTO with a double arrow pointing toward the right. Martin soon interprets it: "It is more than time for you to make a complete change of direction toward the right in your life." Meaning that he thinks Lisbeth should stop to look all around her and concentrate on the group and her spiritual journey under his guidance to become a well-trained soldier of the Sixth Race to save humanity from destruction. But is this a right or left turn? It all depends where you stand!

Since survival is a basic need on the Maslow scale, one has to work to get money to ensure food and shelter, whatever Martin can think about it. Consequently, when Lisbeth gets a phone call from the hiring agency, she accepts the short-term job in a catholic institution. She'll just have to correct and type a large document which happens to be the story of the foundation of this establisment. And she finds it quite interesting. While she is reviewing the text, the human resources manager comes to her with a sigh of satisfaction that she did the work so professionally in such a short time. He recognizes Lisbeth's potential as being valuable and asks her if she wants to work full-time. Of course, she does. He then tells her that the position is presently available as a secretary to the Director of the institution. If she is interested, she just has to prepare her résumé with an introductory letter mentioning her motivation to get the job and send the whole thing to the named authorities. No sooner said than done: the letter says that she would really like to work there because the ambiance she felt is one of spiritual peace and contemplation. As soon as they receive the letter, they call her back saying that the job is hers and she can start this very next Monday.

Lisbeth is very happy and she praises the Lord for answering her prayers. She also calls Martin to give him the news. He seems to rejoice too and he says: "You see, when you make the necessary efforts, things happen: it is the law of return. Now, let's see how long it will last." Lisbeth wonders why he added this negative comment but it won't stop her. And she will not prove him right! So, on this special Monday, she is there as one. And she'll have to learn on the spot, all by herself, because the woman who was doing the job has left over a month ago and is thus unable to give her any training whatsoever. The challenge is even more motivating for Lisbeth and she is ready to catch up with the work. This job, as she feels it, will give her financial security and help her get back an emotional equilibrium, in a spiritual environment filled with the presence of God. It doesn't take long for her to link this happening with the PRONTO sign she saw just a little while ago. The arrow was pointing exactly that way.

For the time being, Lisbeth doesn't socialize much with the rest of the staff there and during the coffee break periods, she goes to the small chapel they showed her at the end of the hallway. There, alone before God, in silence and tranquillity, she suddenly recognizes what she had been searching: a profound serenity, a peaceful spiritual inner well-being. She feels it deep inside her; it's almost tangible. She is absolutely sure of her feeling: it is great and it is exactly what she longed for all these past years. She was searching outside of her, in the group, with the master, what was simply hidden inside her. It is the divine Presence! She now feels it so strong and so deep in her heart, in her soul, in her whole being. And it feels so good!

During her following meeting with Martin, she is all enthusiasm telling him about that wonderful spiritual revelation. The man shows some kind of approval but he cannot forget the mission he gave himself to fight and destroy the negative entities around him and around his disciples. He again attacks Pauline to try and get out of her mouth the words that will confirm the forms because, says he, he can see a form behind her, a shining red humanoid shape with horns reflected in the window behind her. Since it is dark outside, the window acts as a mirror. And he swears Pauline is that evil customer he sees; he even affirms she is the devil himself.

Suddenly feeling a new strong energy acting inside her, Lisbeth answers: "No! That is not me. I am Lisbeth, a child of God! I might not be perfect but I am not the devil! NO! NO! NO!" She is now crying with soft tears of relief; it took her a great effort to make this firm statement. And Martin does not like it at all. He starts accusing her of all kinds of faults, he even says he feels like hitting her physically. He is angry because, says he, she is abusing him, taking his energy away, fighting against him and refusing to cooperate. He won't hit her though because he can see the words, clearly written in Lisbeth's eyes: DON'T YOU DARE!

Another incident irritates Martin: Lisbeth has neglected some parts of the requested discipline and skipped a few exercices because she doesn't feel at ease with them. The rules ask the disciples to meditate everyday, invoking the cosmic forces, a different one for each different day of the week. For example, Saturday, they have to call on Saturn, Sunday it is the Sun; Monday the moon, etc. Lisbeth doesn't feel comfortable with this rule anymore and Martin cannot accept her refractory behavior. He suddenly regains control over his anger and directs their conversation on her new job: "Everything seems under control and positive for you. You love your new job, you work full-time and get a good pay; you like the ambiance and everything. But, you cannot keep this job and continue with the group. You have to choose."

Lisbeth is shocked; she is not sure she heard right. Yes, her scale of values has been quite disturbed during the last few months but she still has enough good sense to realize that these two alternatives are not equivalent on the balance. It simply has no logic and she is stunned. With a puzzled sarcastic smile, she replies: "This is not logical!" Martin confirms: "Yes, it is a choice I am asking you to make. You have to choose the group or the job. You can take a few days to think it over and give me your answer later or you can decide now." Of course, she is working for a priest and of course, during this past week, she personally consulted another priest for her own sake. Is it the main cause of Martin's fury toward her?

For the time being, she is just puzzled at his reaction and, still finding it kind of ridiculous, she promptly replies: "Well then, if these are the two alternatives, my choice is easy to make. I have to work to survive and I am going to keep this job."–"So, then, it means you are going to leave the group ..." Martin comments harshly. Actually a little bewildered by the tone of his voice, she confirms her choice: yes, she will leave the group. "Perfect!" Martin replies rubbing his hands together. "You will come to next Sunday's meeting and we'll give you a few things. Just give me the cross pendant and the opal ring back and keep the crystal pendant for now. we'll give you other instructions later. Farewell. We might meet again some day!"

Lisbeth feels pushed away and leaves. She is crying but she doesn't know why. Does she feel relieved? Is she afraid to find herself alone, abandoned, without friends? Is she scared that all the promised damnation spells will materialize? Or is she crying with the premonitive joy of getting her God-given freedom back? She doesn't really know but she lets the tears go down abundantly, thus relieving a heavy load from her heart.

Yet these tears are nothing compared to what she goes through on the following Sunday. Still submitted to Martin's command, she is present at the group meeting and today, she is a chosen target. Numerous arrows are thrown at her without hesitation. Martin starts first; he prepared an incriminating speech which he shouts at her with a poisoned-dart tone of voice. Never before in her life as Lisbeth feels so tiny, so humiliated, so repressed, so mortified. The master shamelessly unveils some intimate secrets Lisbeth had talked about in her personal encounter with him. It is a profanation of professional confidence, a serious fault against the basic code of ethics. He really wants Lisbeth to feel cheap and unworthy of respect. He even heaps his own personal reproaches on her, throwing all kinds of bad spells at her in a spirit of revenge. It is really too much; it is simply unhuman and Lisbeth cannot understand such cruelty.

Mark is sitting beside Martin across the room, directly facing Lisbeth. Every time she looks at him and meet his eyes, her tears come up even more abundant and painful. She suddenly knows the reason of her sorrow: she is crying over Mark who believes he is under Martin's protection now. This is no protection, this is possession and control. She now knows better: this is not the road to heaven, it is the road to hell. And she is so sorry she got her young friend along in this tortuous journey. She is leaving it today but how is he going to get out of Martin's claws? Deep inside her, she expresses one sincere wish: may Mark come out of there as soon as possible, with as little hurts as possible, through the grace of God!

Lana is already gone: she did not understand much but she took the right decision. Louisa is just about to leave, the two dancers are gone. Chantal's young son felt the absence of love and chose to return with his father and brother. Lisbeth is now leaving with no other regrets than the fact that she has to leave Mark and some other loved ones behind. They just cannot see that they are being manipulated by Martin; under the cover of protection, he knows how to handle and use them for his own purpose. By the way, what is his purpose? To Lisbeth, it is the total opposite of what he first told her: "My master is Christ!" What a false statement! He is more of an antichrist, really! Undercover antichrist! A despicable usurper! He may be sick in his mind but he sure acts it out with a perverse pleasure, making the sour pill look sweet and the darkness look bright! What will become of the other ones still under his spell? What will happen to Celina and her unborn baby? How will he treat these two innocent and helpless creatures? Being conscious of the damage Martin can do, Lisbeth cannot but feel sad, deeply sad about the whole situation. Through the grace of God, she was given enough strength and courage to get out of the trap. May the same grace touch all the others and help them out of this ambush!

We are at the end of January and the first thing Lisbeth wants is to reconcile with her daughters. She is glad to be free of Martin's grip and from now on, she will follow her own heart and feelings. Her children are her priority and she loves them sincerely. Yann always remained with her but it doesn't mean he didn't suffer. Sarah is back with her but the relationship was quite distant and cold these past few months. Vicky lives in her apartment with friends but she also needs comforting. Lisbeth is ready to ask forgiveness for all the sufferings she caused her three children and she does it, no matter how long it will take for them to forgive. The main thing is that she really is repentant: she sincerely regrets and she is deeply sorry. She also knows that she was manipulated into that process; it was not done on her own will; her true power had been taken away for a time. Of course, she is responsible for letting Martin influence her judgement but until just lately, she was not aware of the amplitude it had taken.

Two weeks later, she is convicted to a meeting with the group, along with her three children. She has to be there in the morning and the children are to join her in the afternoon. The reason is that Martin wants to give her a gift as a souvenir of her short stay, of her effort to integrate the group, her attempt to become a soldier of the Sixth Race. The gift she receives at the beginning of the meeting is a silver cross without the corpus. Then, the meeting goes on as usual: Lisbeth does not participate actively, she is just being a spectator. After a moment of silence and a few invocations of the universal energies, it's just the usual routine. Except that today, Lisbeth sees everything with new eyes, and can better identify the irregularities. First, there never was a Sign of the cross performed in the meetings … she used to do it secretly inside herself but could not make the link between her intuition and her mind as to why, in a gathering of christian people, this was willingly omitted. Something was blocking her awareness. With her newly recovered clearness of mind, she can also see the underlying message of the words Martin invites her and the rest of the group to write down so as to remember them forever.

Read this message for yourself and discover how incongruous, or revealing it is:

> *Just by looking at the attitudes and actions of those who fight, we can easily identify their motivation. Those who work for God are peaceful and they act with wisdom, charity and love while the others attack with passion, hatredness and violence.*
>
> *On this day, I face this huge responsibilty of mine and I become conscious of my actions, my thoughts and my words. For the rest of my life on earth, I will call on the law of return and be totally accountable for it.*
>
> *This Full-Moon Sunday of February 1983.*

When Vicky, Sarah and Yann join in, Martin concentrates his attention on them. To each one individually, he predicts all the problems they'll have to face due to their stubbornness, especially the girls, who also have a few positive qualities they'll have to use. As for Yann, he predicts a bright future as long as he goes on using his tremendous potential; even Martin himself finds Yann strong, intelligent and witty. The girls want to leave; they don't feel comfortable with so many eyes staring at them, so many cold faces trying to grasp all the energy they can get out of their visitors. Martin tells Sarah that, someday, she might receive a ring made out of her parents wedding rings but that the time has not come yet. After these words, the two girls ask permission to leave and they are followed by their brother.

Then, Lisbeth asks permission to talk as she prepared a special message for each one in the group. She reads it out loud and gives a copy to Martin. How do they receive her loving message? She will never know because they all remain placid, cold as ice, as if all dead already. She concludes addressing Martin, encouraging him to go on passionately with his mission until the Good Lord shows him another road, which she is sure will happen. When she is finished with her words of farewell, she dares ask Martin to give her back the jewellery he took away from her. She'll accept it no matter the shape he gave it. After all, it was Martin's promise to give her back her smoked topaze ring. But her request is considered too audacious, indecent even, and Martin reacts furiously: "What? After all what we did for you, you dare ask for more? After all the fights we went through in order to free you from slavery? After all the energies we spent for you, you dare ask for more? What will you require next? Our blood? You are unworthy of wearing even that pure silver cross we gave you this morning! You would tarnish it! We thus ask you to take it off and to deposit it on the floor in the middle of the room, along with the crystal we had left you through kindness. And then, you can leave. We are through with you and with your children. You really deserve each other. And good luck! You'll need it!"

Lisbeth is crying a little, mostly because she is astonished at Martin's violent reaction to what she considers a very legitimate request. She doesn't understand but now, she doesn't want to understand. Contrasting Martin's brutality, she gets up slowly, she calmly takes the cross and crystal off her neck and places them on the cushion in the center of the room. Walking toward the door, she gives a quick look around as a farewell to all and a last profound glance to Mark that she will see later at the apartment. And she leaves this infernal place forever.

What a relief she feels. She is broken-hearted about Mark but so glad to be out of Martin's torturing clutches. How could this man be so false on their first encounter and pretend he was a disciple of Christ? Not even once could she recognize Christ's ways during these past months of so-called spiritual journey. The usurper did his best to crush her and make her follow him in his way to hell but he did not succeed. Thanks God that Thou art the Strongest and Thou deliver us from evil. Thanks to the prayers of the numerous persons who loved and still love Lisbeth. Thanks to the silent work of the Lord Who found her a job among his People. Now, she can heal her wounds and rebuild her self-esteem with the help of her real friends, the ones who really wants her well-being and her happiness.

When she feels better, she calls Steve, her beloved, telling him the good news that she is out of the infernal process and at peace in her heart and soul. But not completely free yet as she has to recuperate the famous Buddha and wear it for a whole year, according to Martin's request transmitted through Mark. Steve will send it to her but she won't wear it: it will be turned into ashes by the hands of the good priest she is consulting and who is now helping her to recover her emotional and spiritual balance. She prays that her young friend Mark be soon freed from Martin's malevolent grasp.

The usurper managed to get Lana out of Mark's life and he is now taking him away from Lisbeth's influence. In time, Mark will leave the group when he least expect it. Really, he didn't see it coming. So trusting in Martin's rightousness and love toward him, Mark was subtly being manipulated. As skinny as a bone, as lost and helpless as a robot, as confused as a zombie, as hollow as an empty shell, he will be sent back to his puzzled parents and Lisbeth will be left with the responsibility of the lease. But before he leaves, she feels the pressing need to tell him what has happened to him under Martin's guidance. She is now awaken and aware and she wants Mark to know that he has been twisted around like a puppet and is now entangled in the broken strings, with no other bearing, no other resources but his parents. Just a few months under Martin's guardianship and he losts his car, his Hammond organ, his piano, his furniture and his identity. Lisbeth feels deep compassion for him and for his loving parents who are completely devastated at the sight of him. She understands their eagerness to take him away from this morbid situation.

Lisbeth is sure Martin gave strict orders to Mark, forbidding all communication between her and his parents. Even if she would like to talk to them, to ask their forgiveness for her share of the responsibility, she will not insist. And on this special Good Friday, she makes her own Way of the Cross; she is carrying her own cross alone, with no one to help her or accompany her up the hill. Not a sigh, not a word of farewell. It is the final act of Martin's play in her life.

CHAPTER 19

▼

LIBERATION

On this particular Good Friday, Lisbeth had planned to join the repentance walk in the streets of the city. But she cannot do it because of Mark's moving out. Now that he has left with whatever few belongings he had left, alone in her apartment, she joins in spirit to the thousands of faithfuls walking Jesus' Way of the Cross. In her heart, she remembers the songs she used to sing in church on that special day and she starts to sing her favorite French hymn called "*Gethsemani*", feeling deep in her soul the meaning of the words: ♪ *When my time comes, you will not understand that I have to die for your salvation, for the forgiveness of your foolishness* ... ♪

Warm, soft tears roll down her cheeks as she continues: ♪ *You will not understand, and you will close your doors, you will close your hearts to my Song of Love* ... ♪ Touching words and melody, indeed! Lisbeth is now crying rivers of tears, healing tears, and she goes on with the song: ♪ ... *and you will go wandering, you, hordes of frightful people, trying to reach some unreachable horizons.* ♪ She cannot go further to sing the chorus, choked that she is with sobbing and emotion, crying her wounds out. She is now aware that, with the group and Martin, she was heading the wrong way, working hard to reach some illusive paradise of spiritual fulfillment. She is so glad to be back on her feet again to walk the right way toward the correct destination. She now finds the adequate words to express what she went through during the past six months: it was a VIOLENT WRENCH. She

just received a sublime and liberating revelation: Christ, that is Jesus being cruci-
fied, is the One and Only, the sacrified Lamb to save humanity. He is the Way,
the Truth and the Life, and she believes in Him.

And today, she borrows saint Thomas' words to express her faith and gratitude:
"*My Lord and my God!*" (Jn 20,28). Such is the song of faithfulness and praise
coming from a converted soul, hoping never to be lost again. Such is Lisbeth's
humble offering of her whole being, body, soul and spirit to the Master of the
Universe: God, Father, Son and Holy Spirit. Forever!

The following week, she returns to church and reintegrates the Christian community with her fellow believers, baptised in the catholic faith inherited from her
family and which answers her needs and thirst for a profound and sincere spiritual journey. Alleluia, o Lord! Alleluia! It is not a matter of coincidence that she
found that job for a catholic institution; it is a miracle, a God-granted grace! And
she appreciates its real value: it really did save her. Now, little by little, she is
reconstructing herself, getting more and more confident in herself and in her
sharpened intuition. No one will ever call her Pauline again. She is Lisbeth, a
child of God, baptised under this sacred name in the catholic church community.

She reconciled with her daughters who are so happy to move back with her and
their young brother. Together again, the four of them really appreciate that the
nightmare is over. Yes, it was a nightmare! Now, only love, time, and the grace of
God will heal the wounds. And since the question of the inheritance has not yet
been settled, whatever money there is left will go to the children, according to
Ralph's will and Lisbeth's heart.

Lisbeth calls Eva, her old-time friend, and Maryan, her mother, to tell them the
good news that she has left the group and the group has left her. Both women
rejoice to this fact: they forgive everything and their relationship is back to what
it was. Many objects have disappeared; many hurts were caused but love and
friendship last through the mishaps of existence. Lisbeth is convinced of this reality because she deeply feels it with her children, with her friend, with her mother
and also with the man she loves over all, Steve. Would she have been burned
alive, she is sure the love she has for him would have survived because "love never
fails" (I Co 13–8). And love is God-given and God is Love.

With her new freedom and well-being, Lisbeth finds her old self again and her inspiration for poetry. And through her deep love for Steve, she feels she can extend her compassion to the whole universe, to all her human brothers and sisters. Her love has become universal and unconditional. That's the way she feels and that the way she expresses it in her own poetic style:

> *To love you is to love the whole humanity*
> *To love you is to discover my true self*
> *To love you enables me to breathe and to sing again*
> *To love you allows me to live anew*
> *Yes, I need to love you for my own survival.*

Conclusion

A few months later, Lisbeth gets a phone call from Mark who finally got out of the group. He almost was dying when, in a moment of panic, he found the strength to break the string that was still holding the crystal gem to his neck and which was strangling him slowly day after day. Even at a distance, Martin was keeping him under his spell. Now Mark feels he can breathe freely again and he is relieved. He is engaged in a family therapy with his parents and a catholic priest who helps them understand what happened and guides them on the way toward a happy life.

Mark also informs Lisbeth that Celina and her young daughter have left the group and are now under the loving care of Celina's parents where she gave birth to another girl (Martin was wrong on that one too!) Her husband Rolland has now left on his own free will. Lisbeth sings yet another Alleluia to praise the Lord for saving his innocent creatures from drowning with Martin's ship.

As for Lisbeth, she still works for the same catholic institution and she lives with her three children. Vicky and Yann go to the same High School, Vicky in Professional Drawing and Printing and Yann in Environmental Science. Sarah is working in a Coffee Shop serving the clients and preparing their orders. They received each their share of their father's legacy: the girls bought themselves some clothes they badly needed and the son bought himself a computer and placed the rest of the money in a savings account at the bank. They all forgave their mother for the detour she made in search of the absolute, of spiritual fulfillment, and they are again a united happy family.

978-0-595-50743-6
0-595-50743-3